FAIRY TREE HOUSE

Coloring Book for Adult

✓ 70 coloring pages
✓ Coloring book for adults
✓ Ideal for colored pencils or markers
✓ Large print page format: 8.5 x 11 inches
✓ High quality
✓ Single-sided pages to avoid spills, ensuring your masterpieces stay clean
✓ Calming and relaxing activity to explore creativity
✓ Reduces stress and anxiety

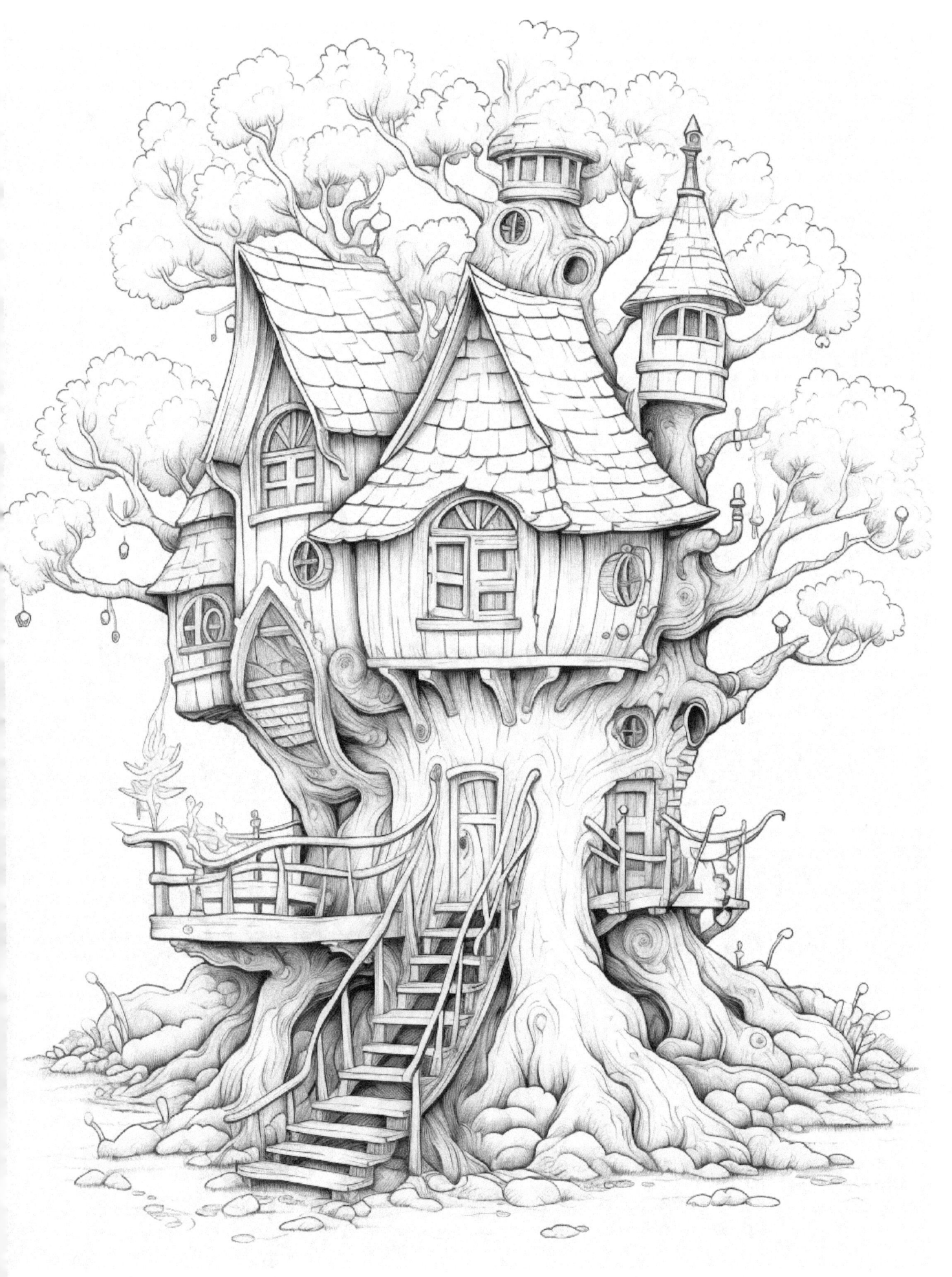

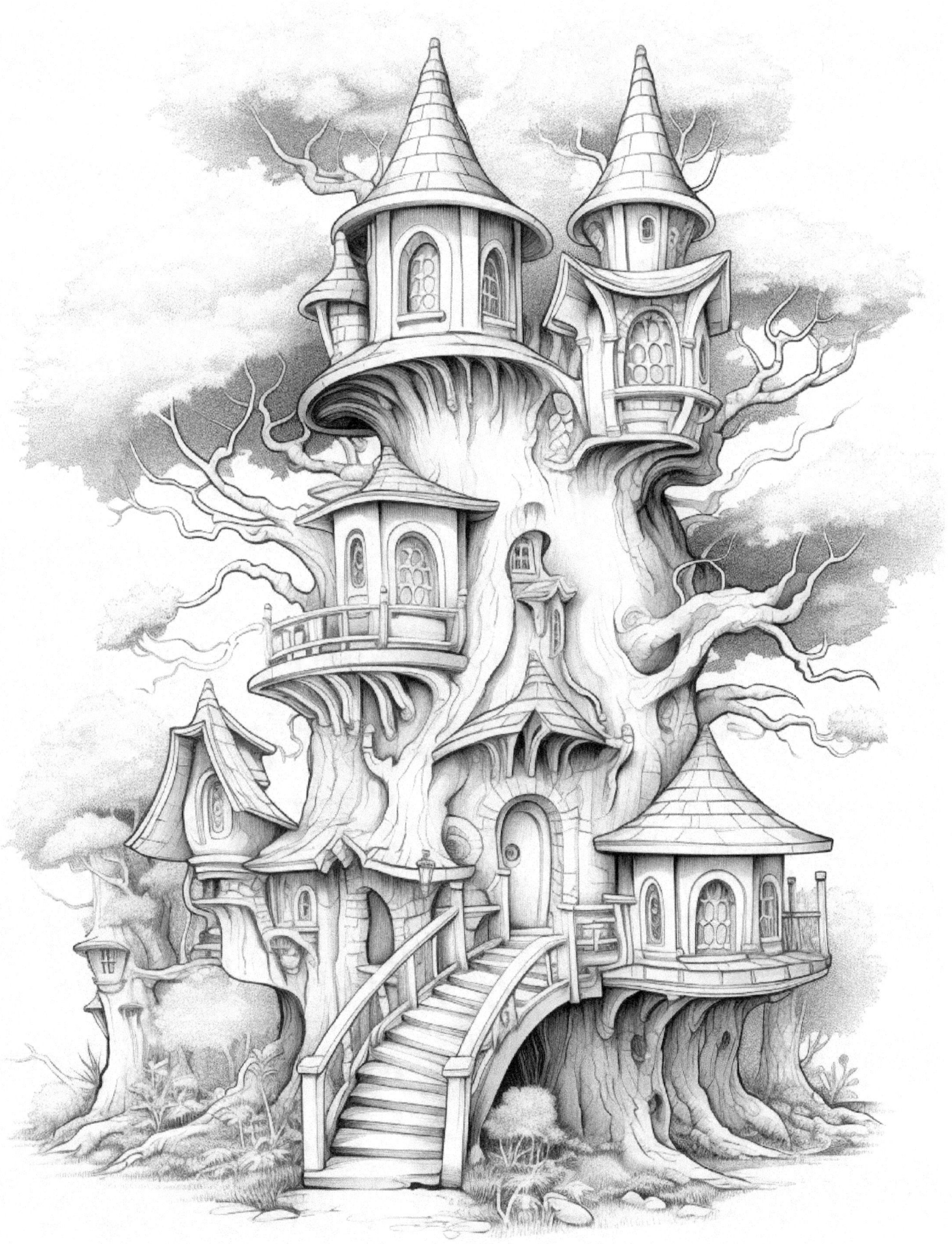

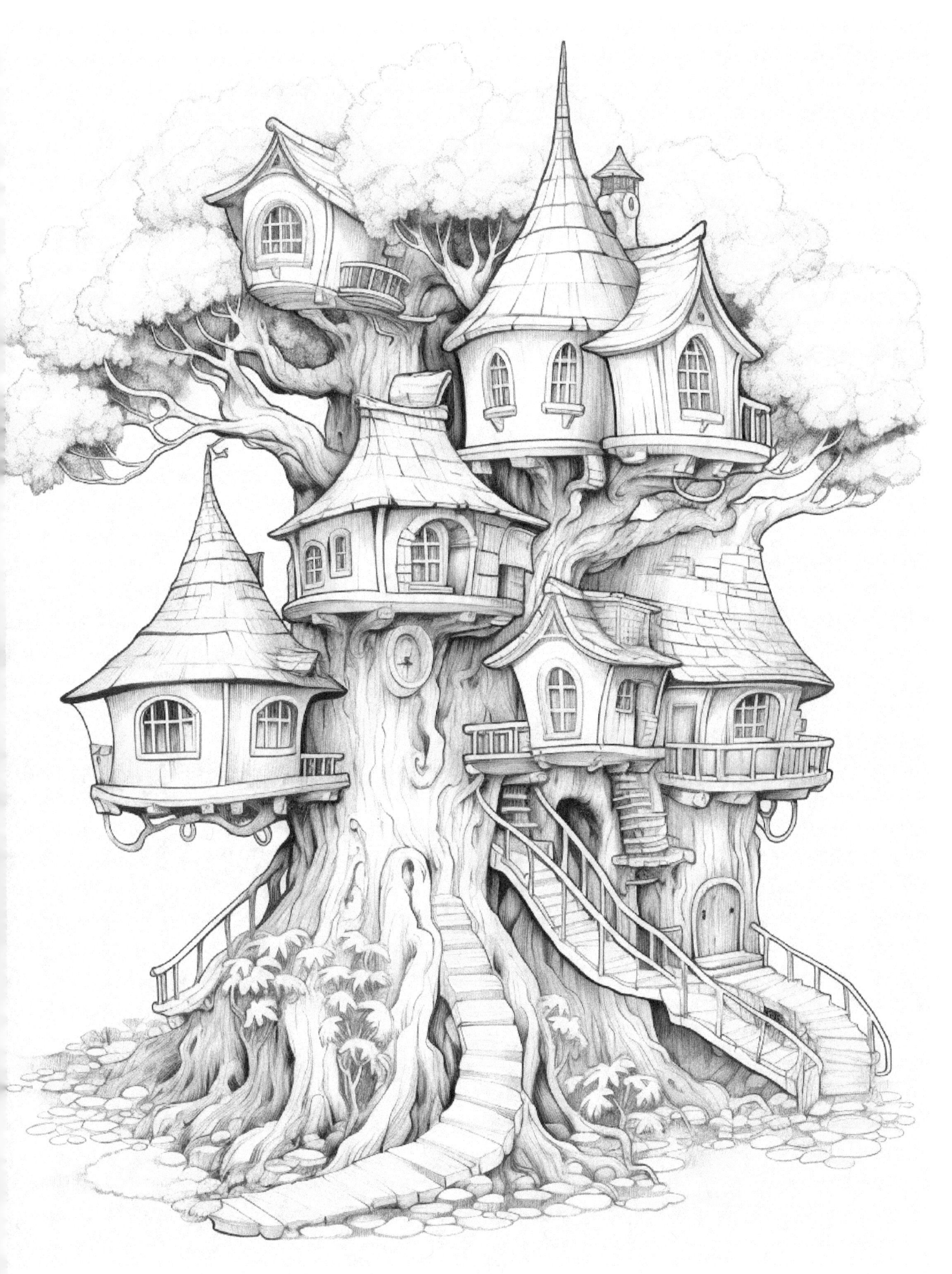

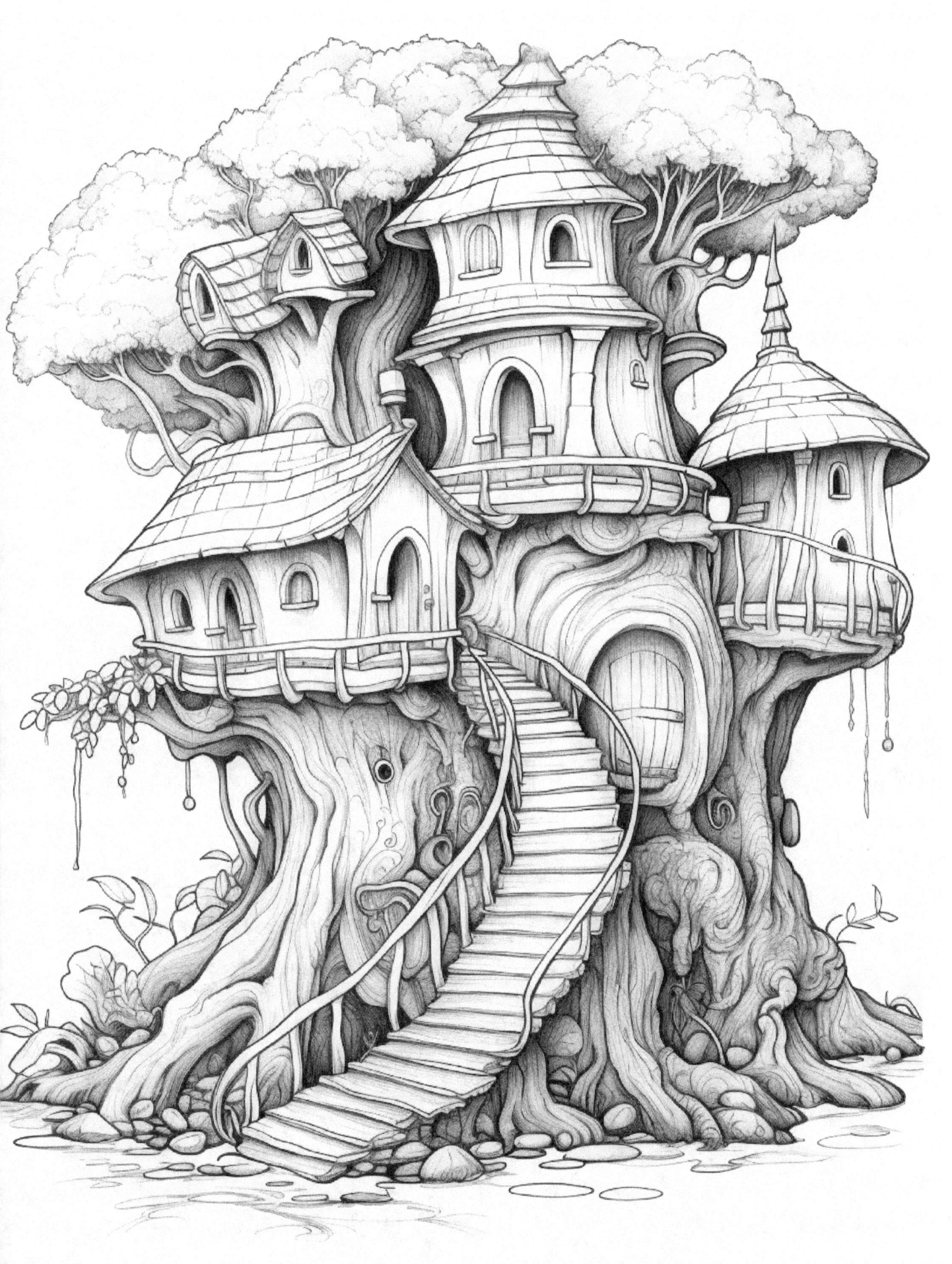

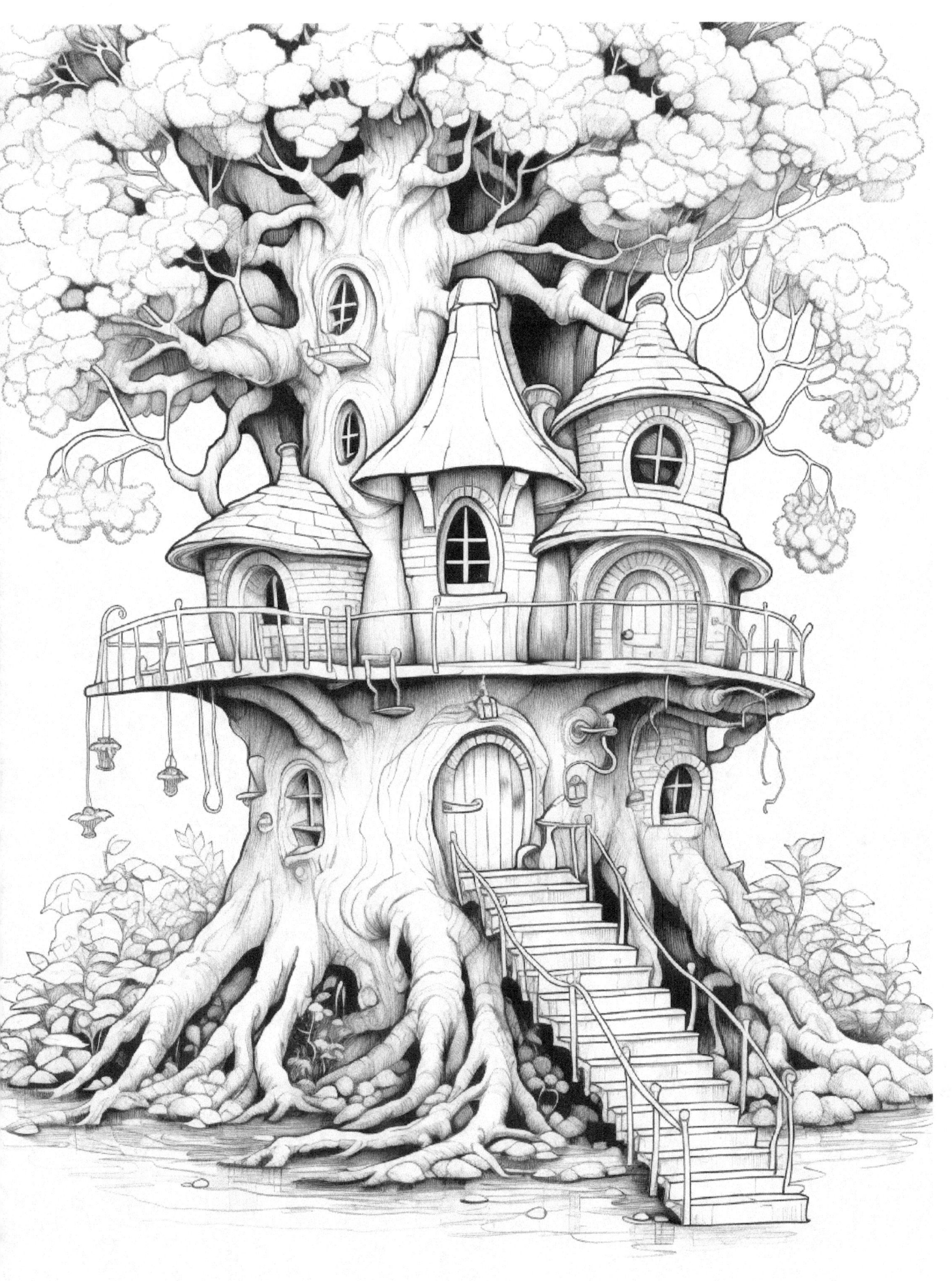

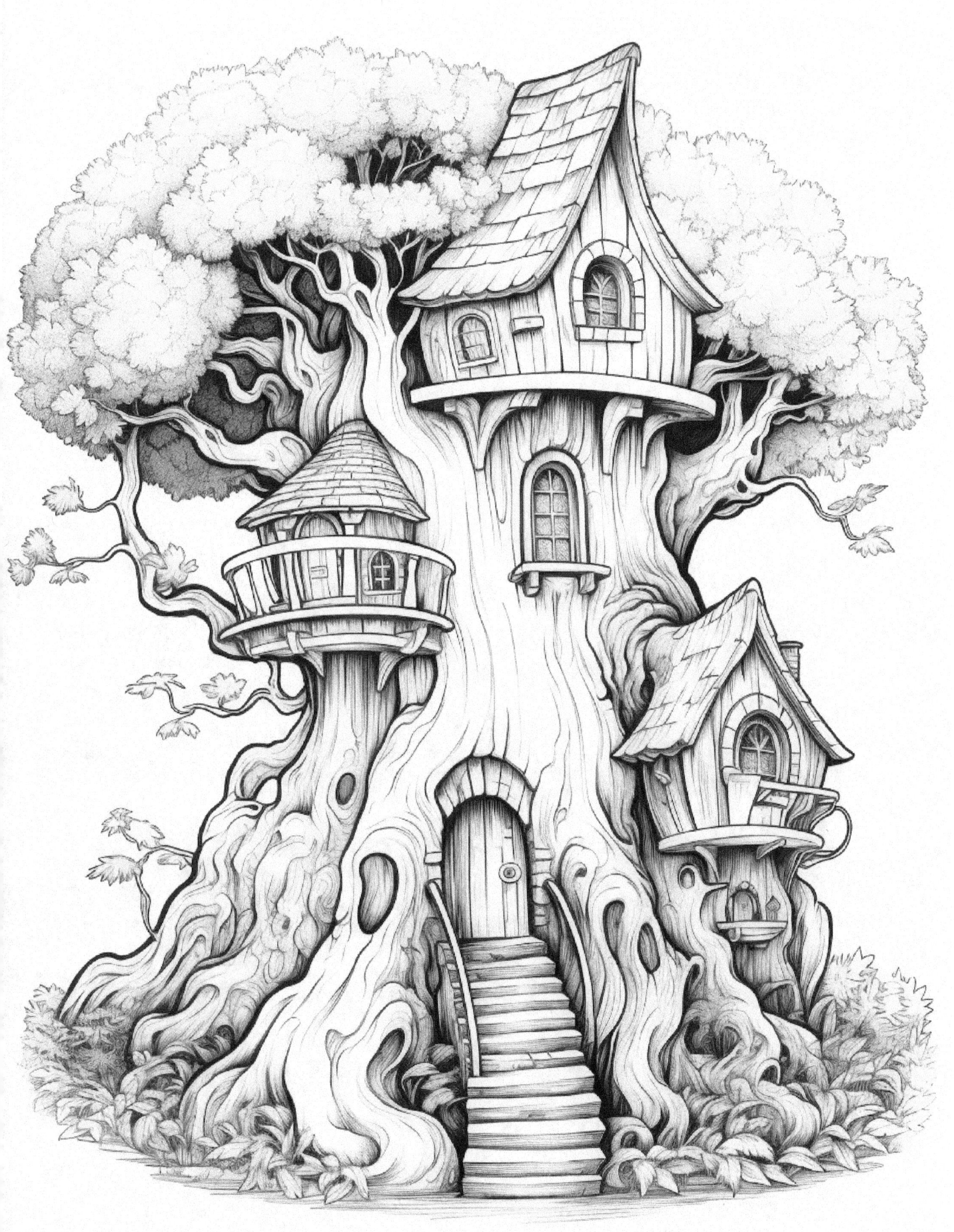

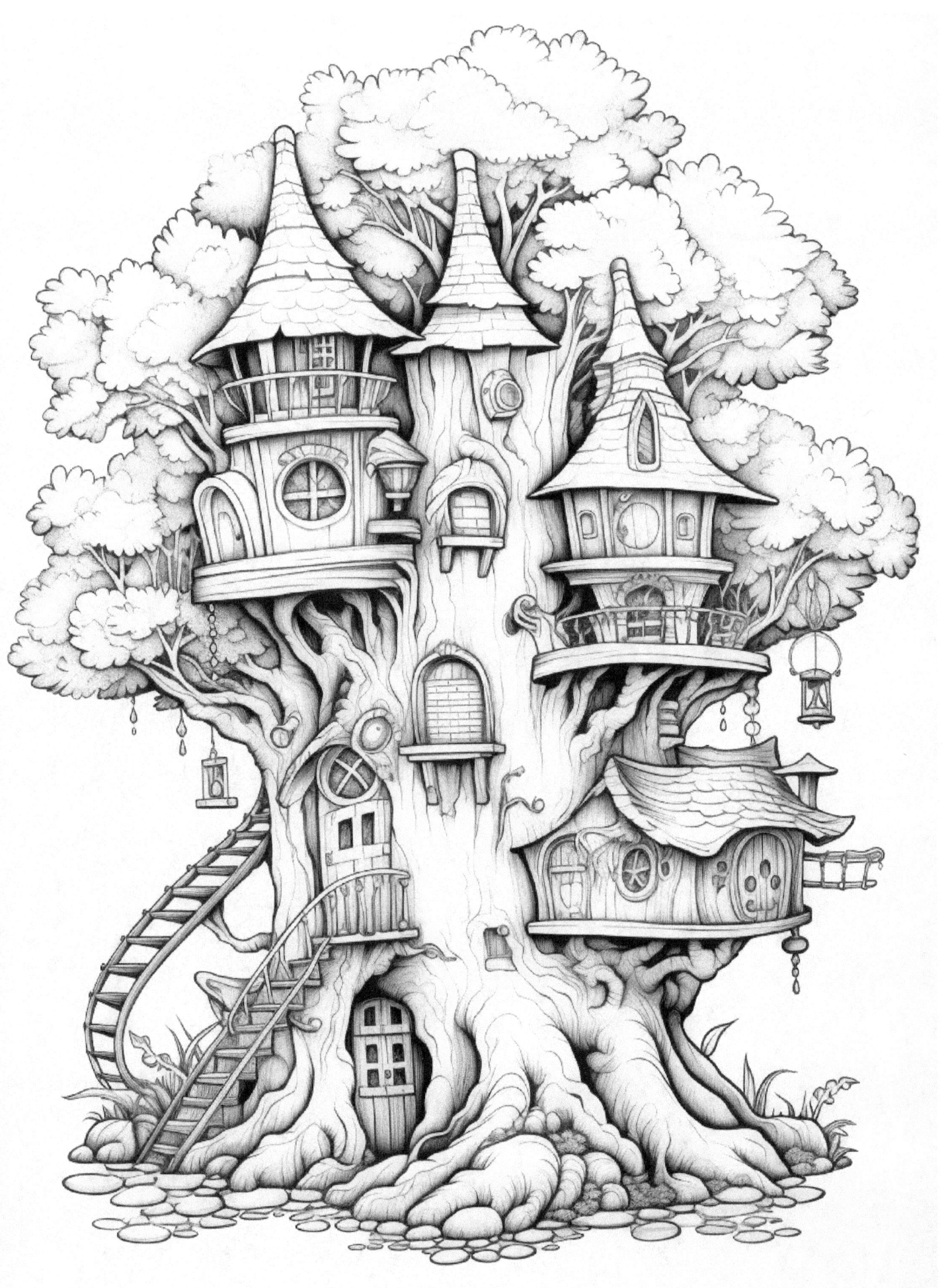

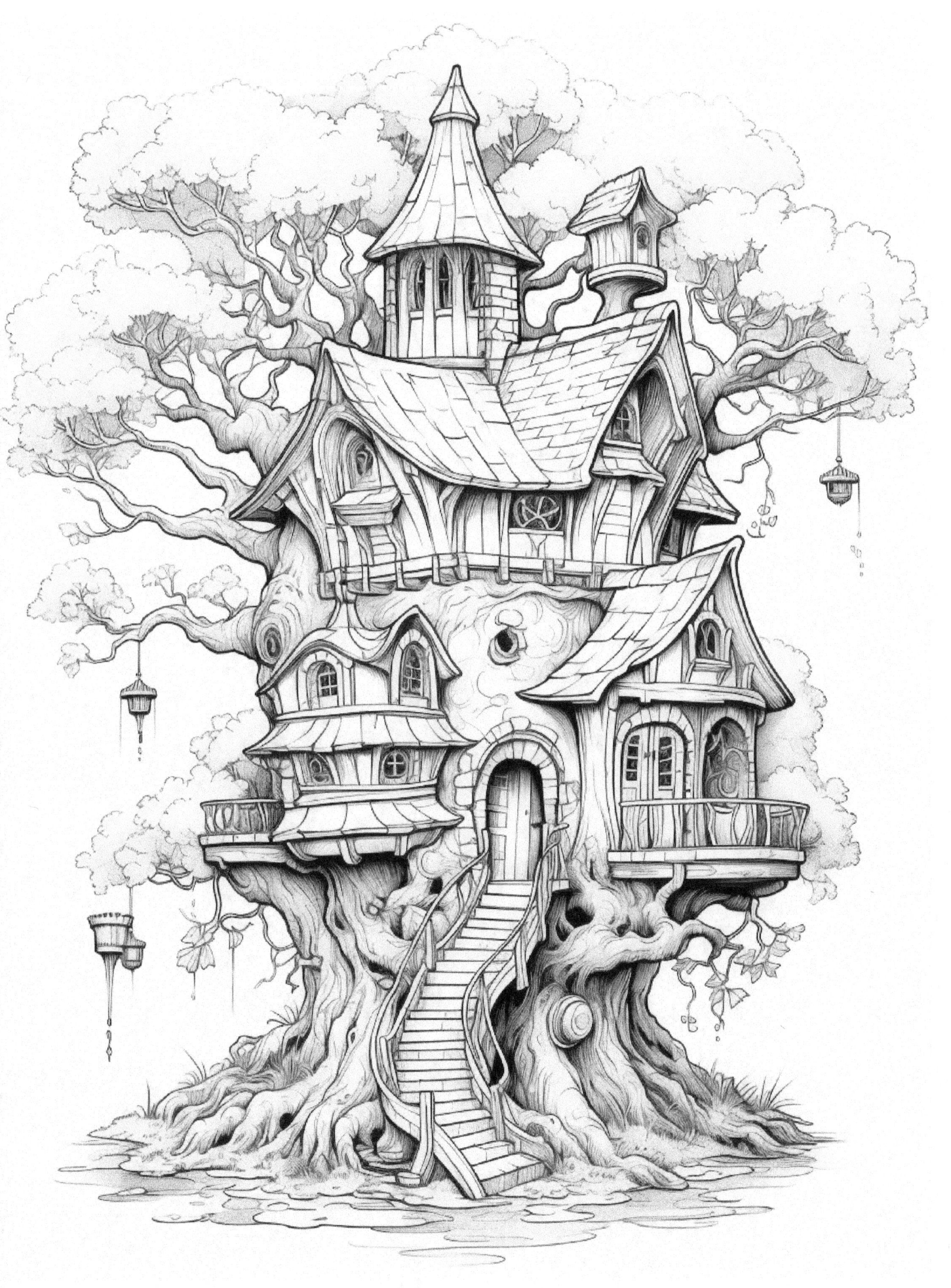

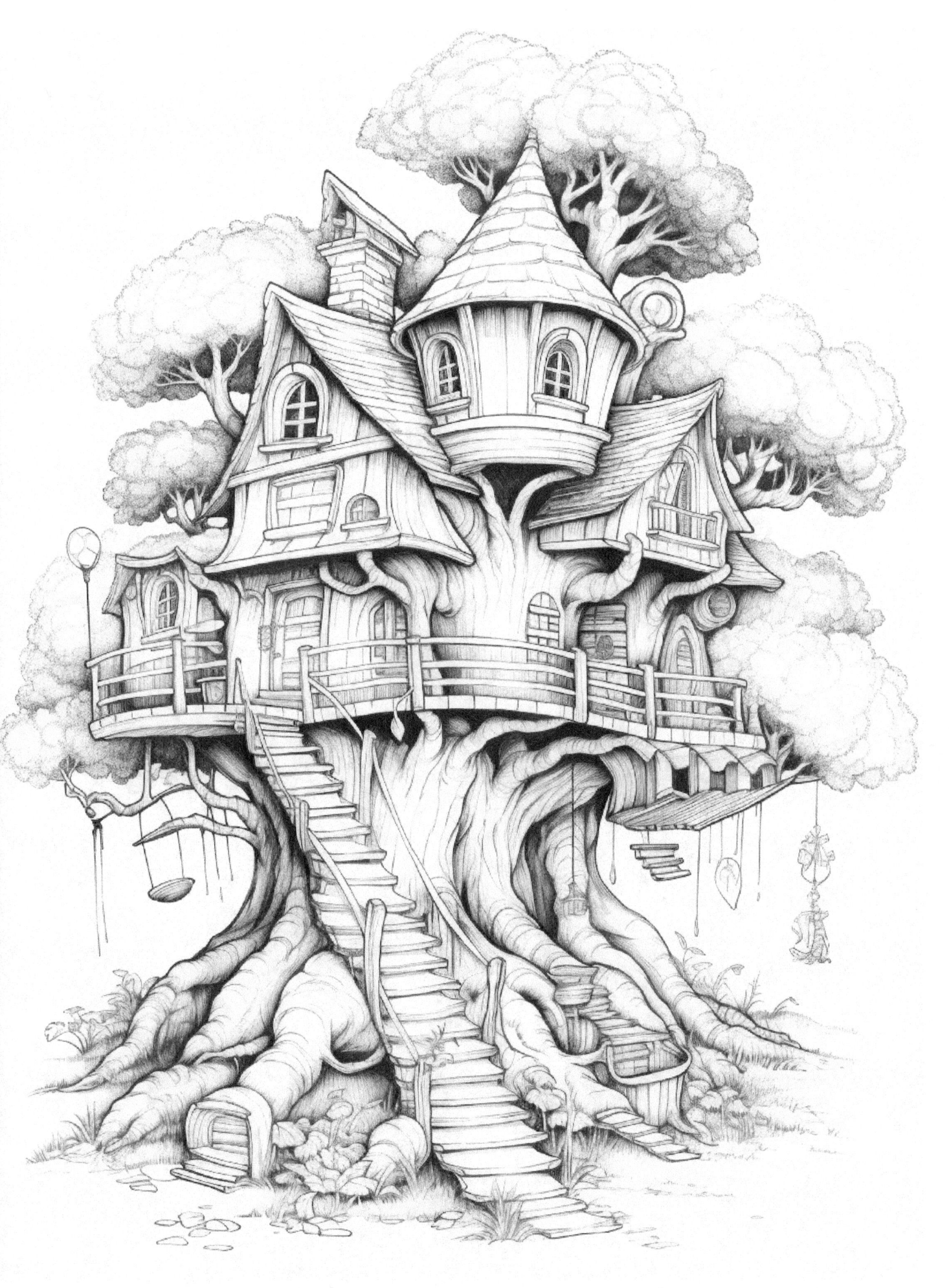

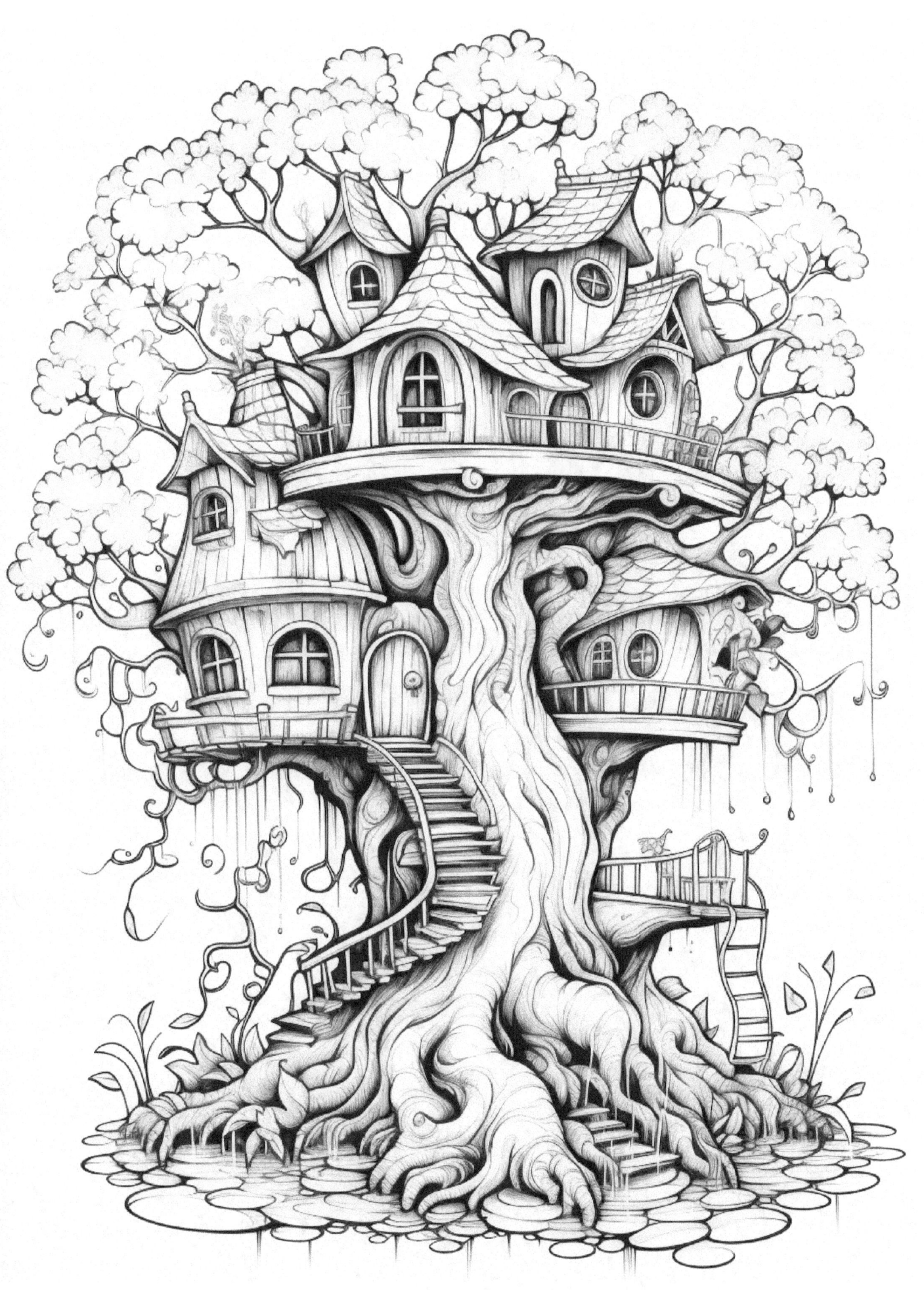

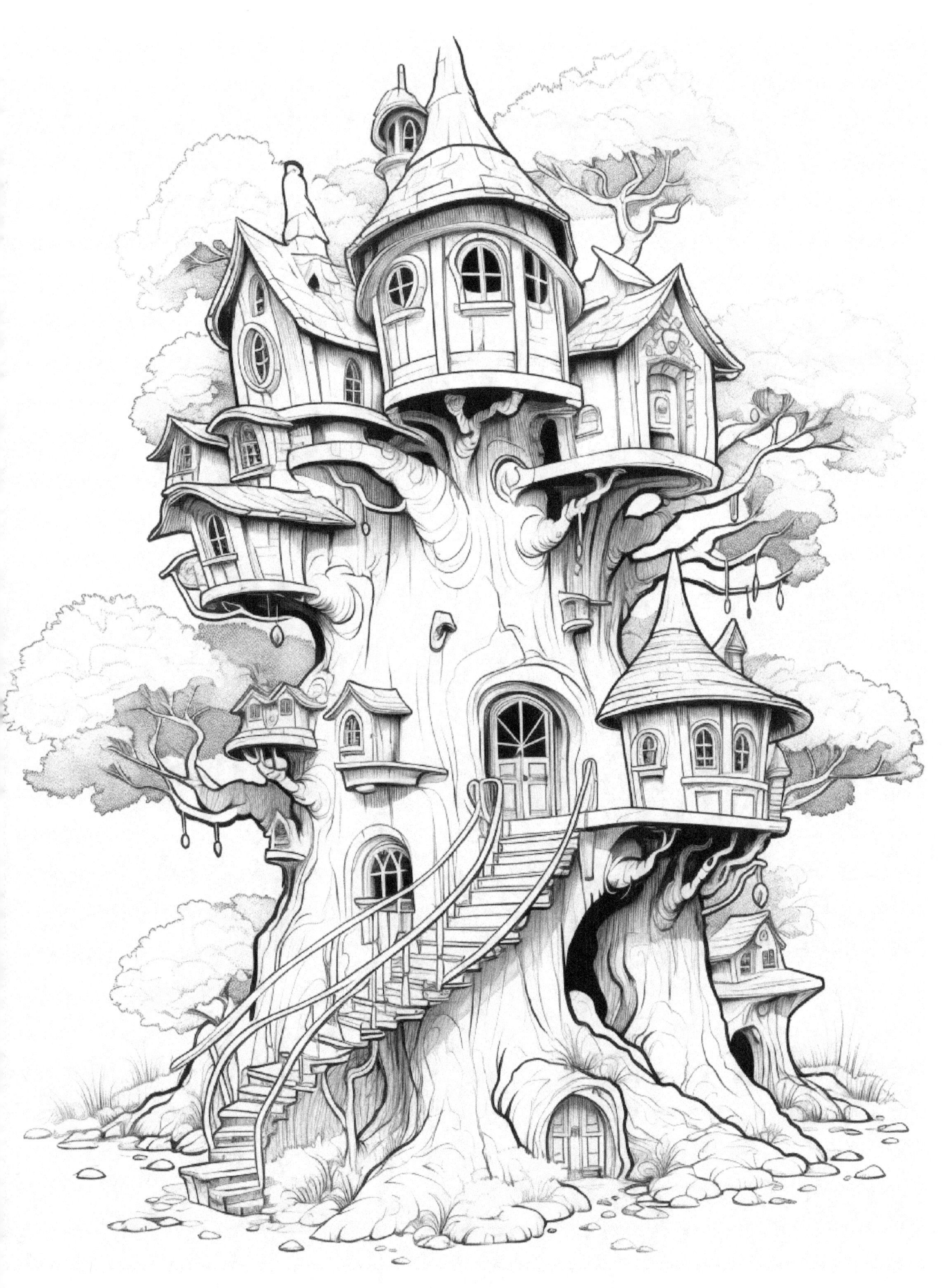

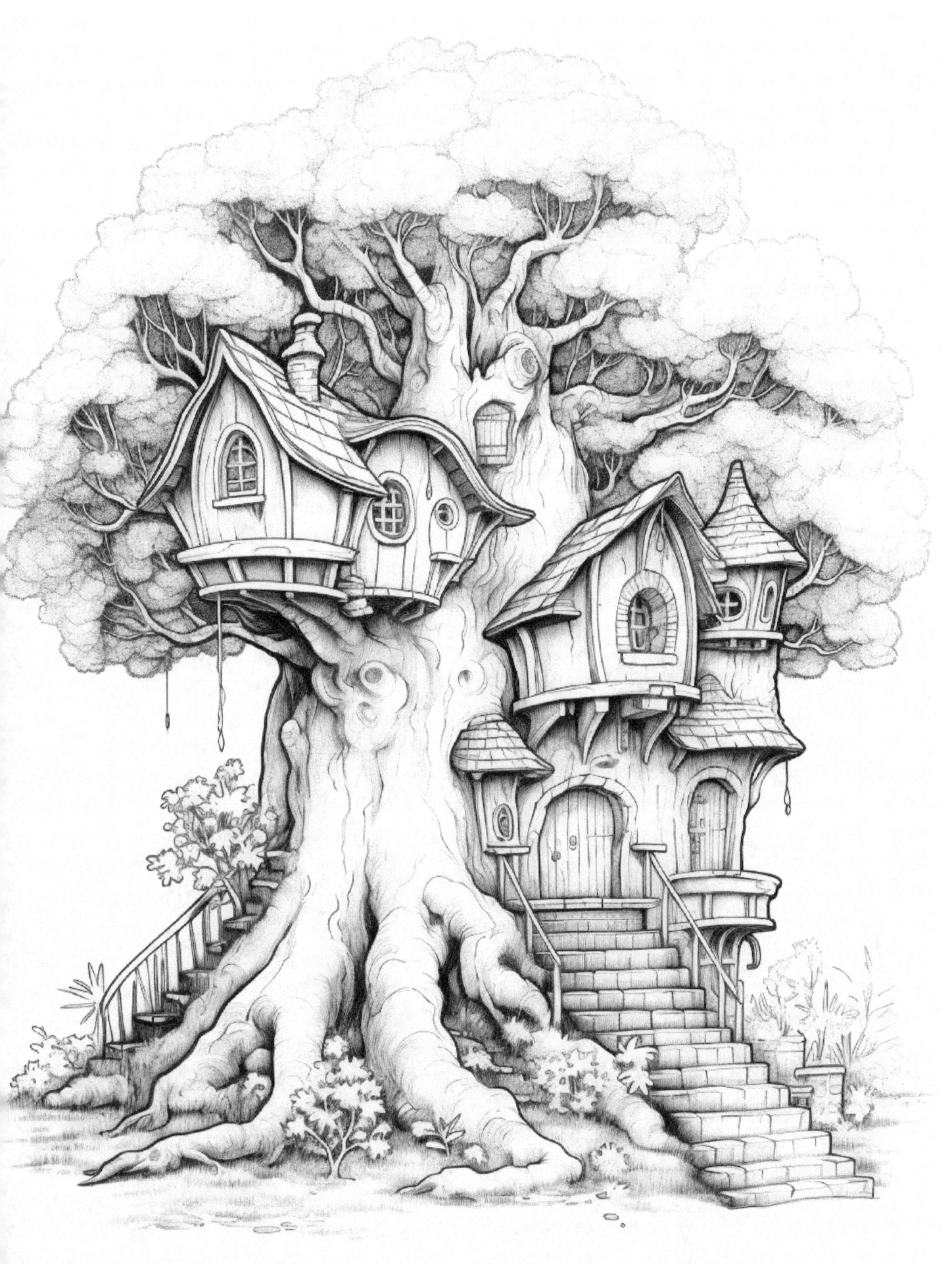

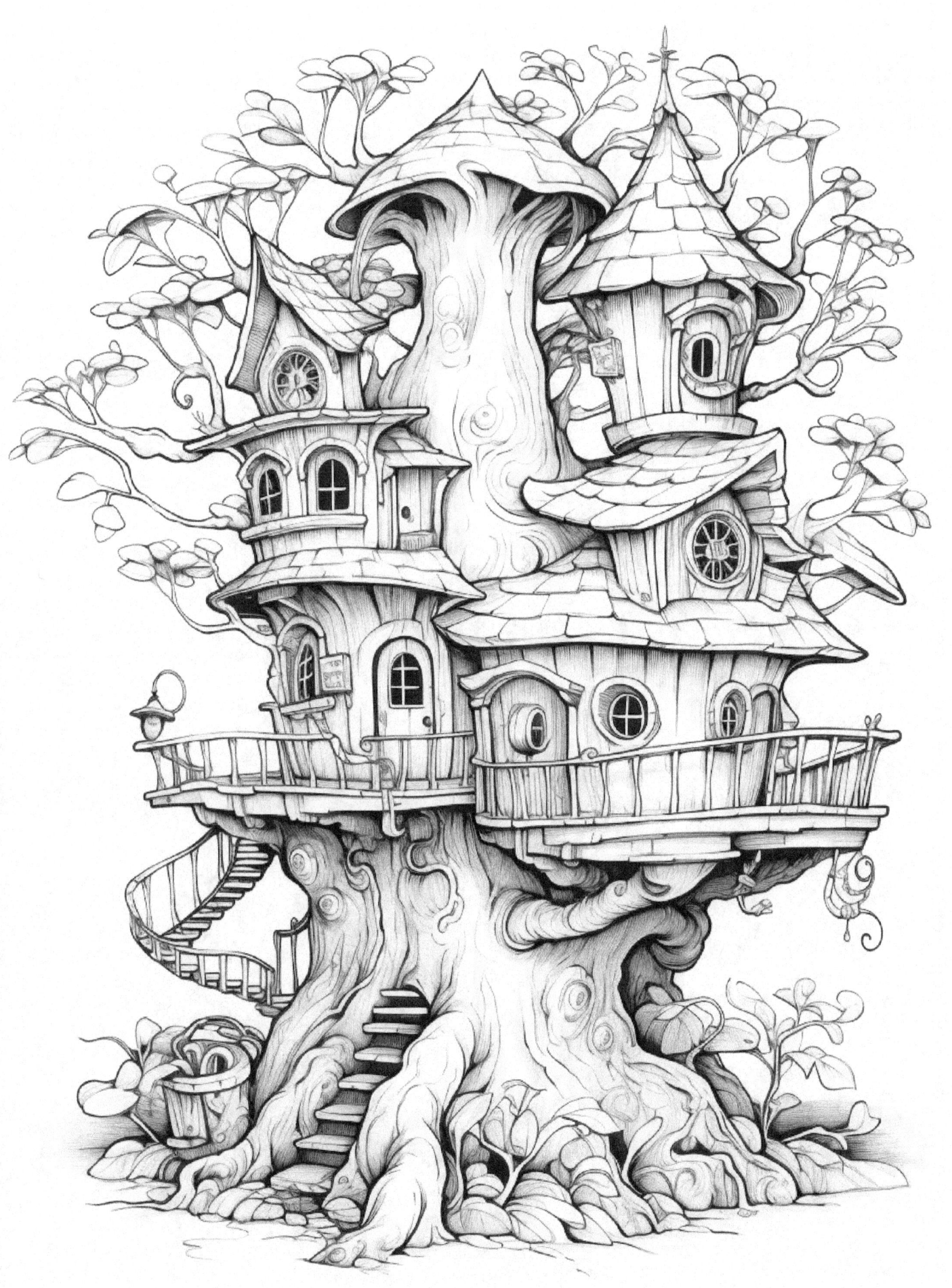

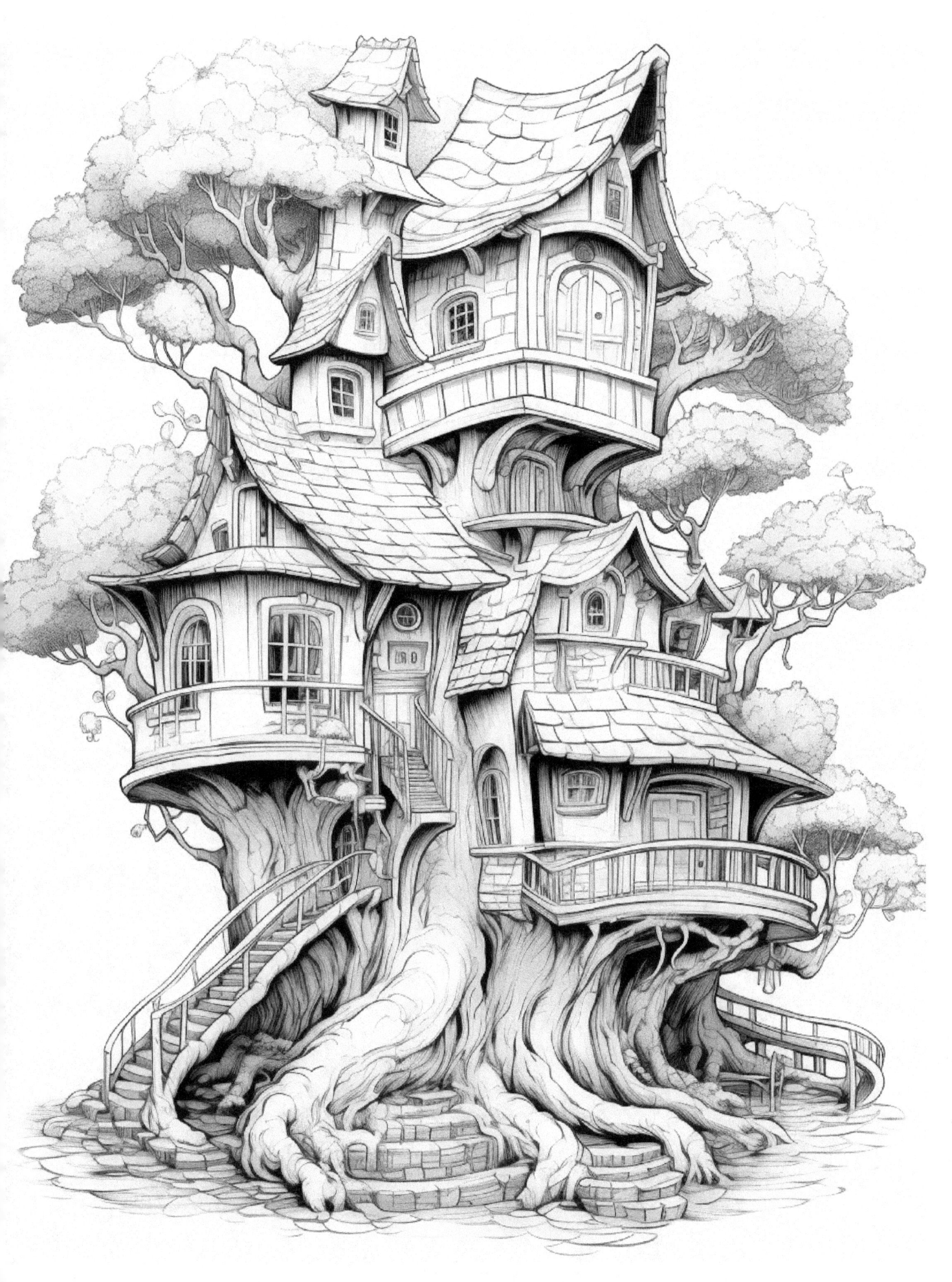

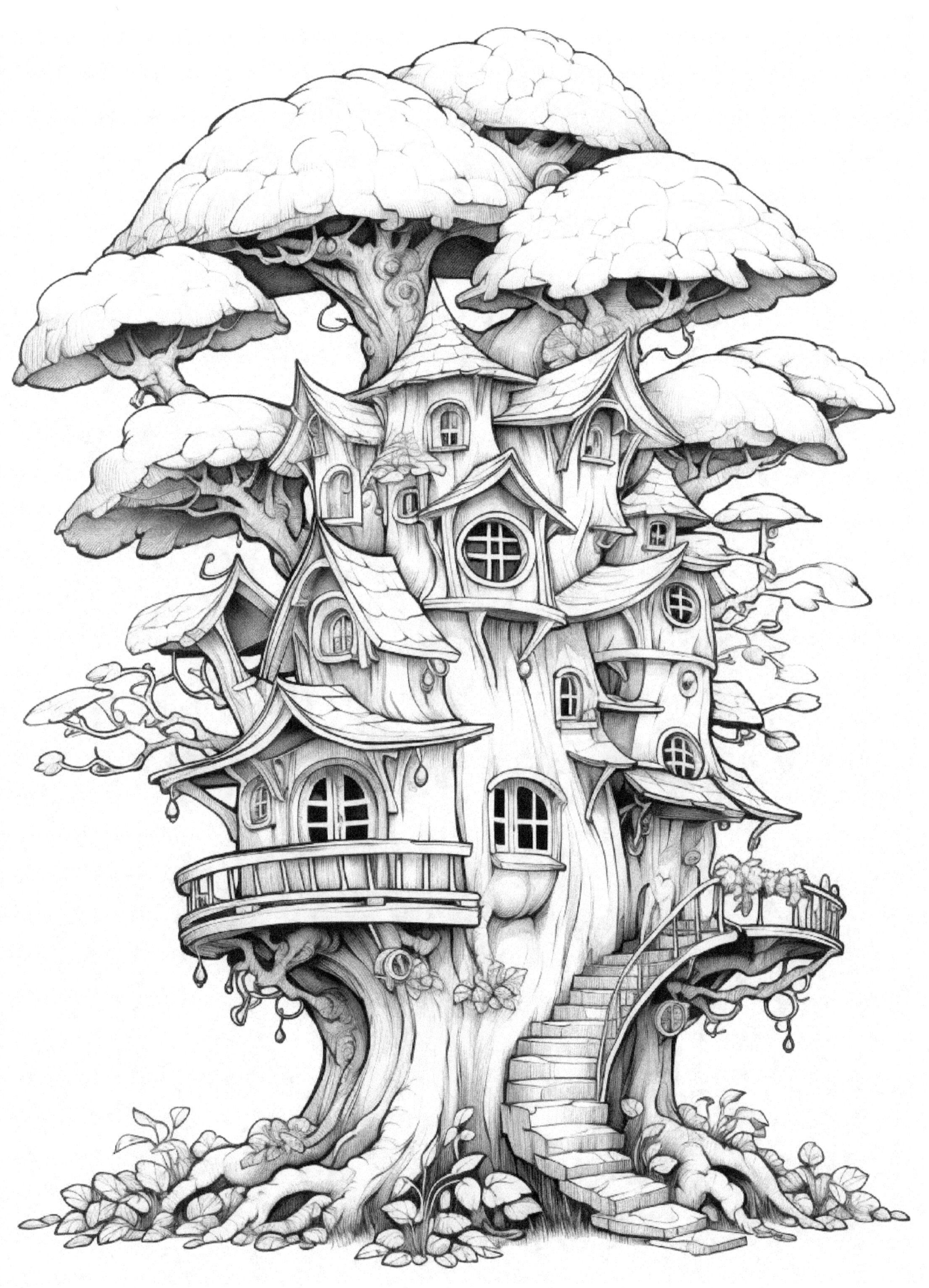

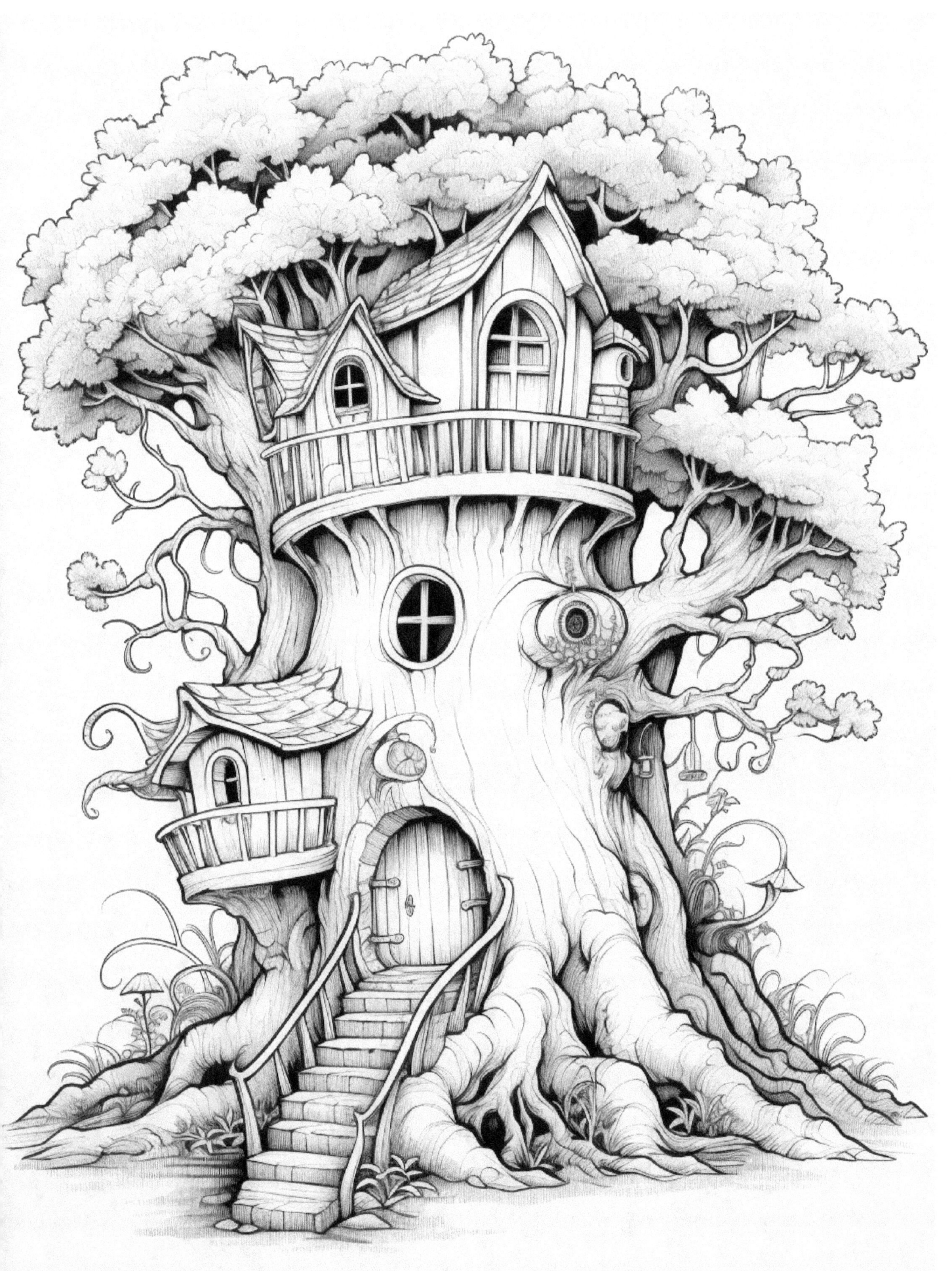

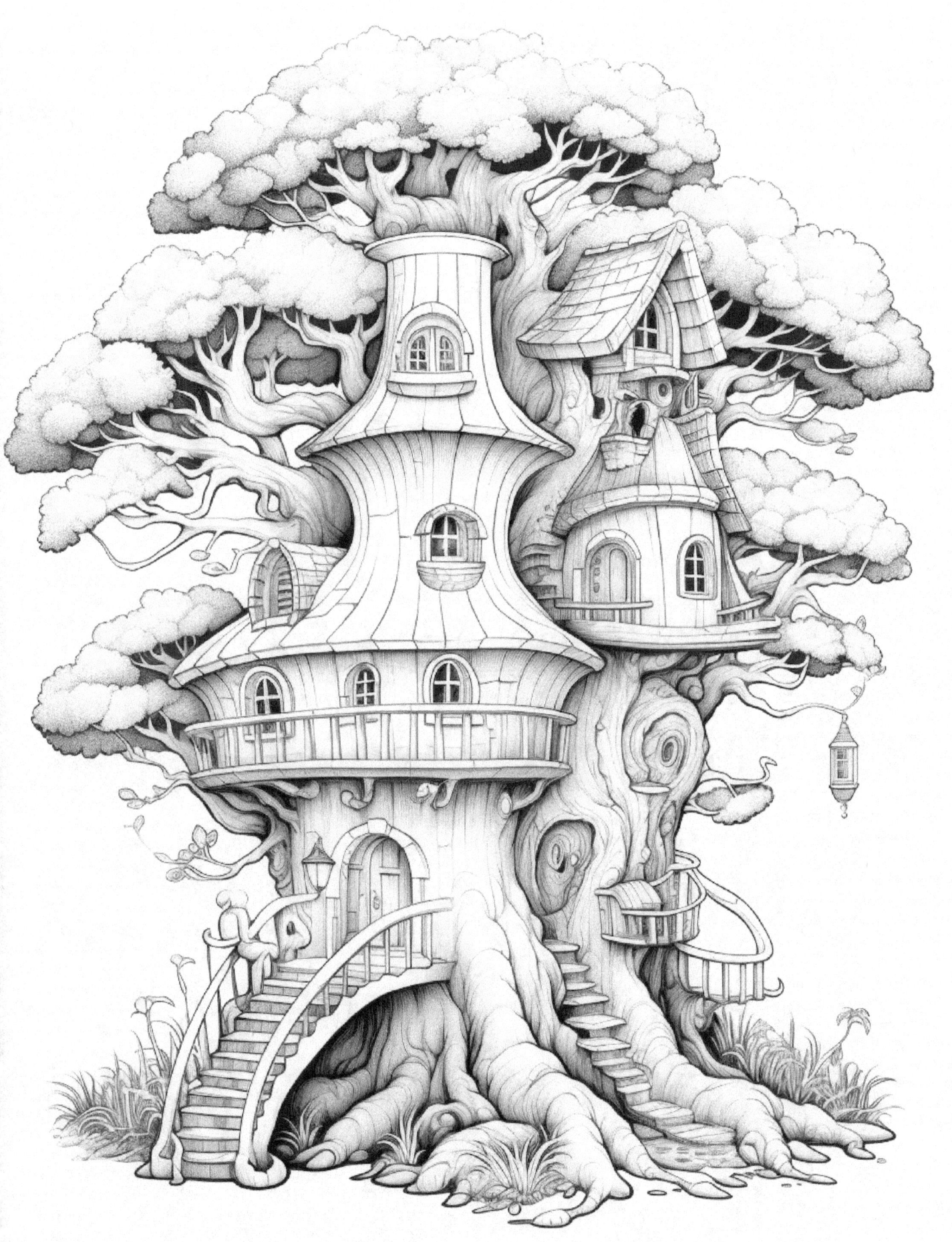

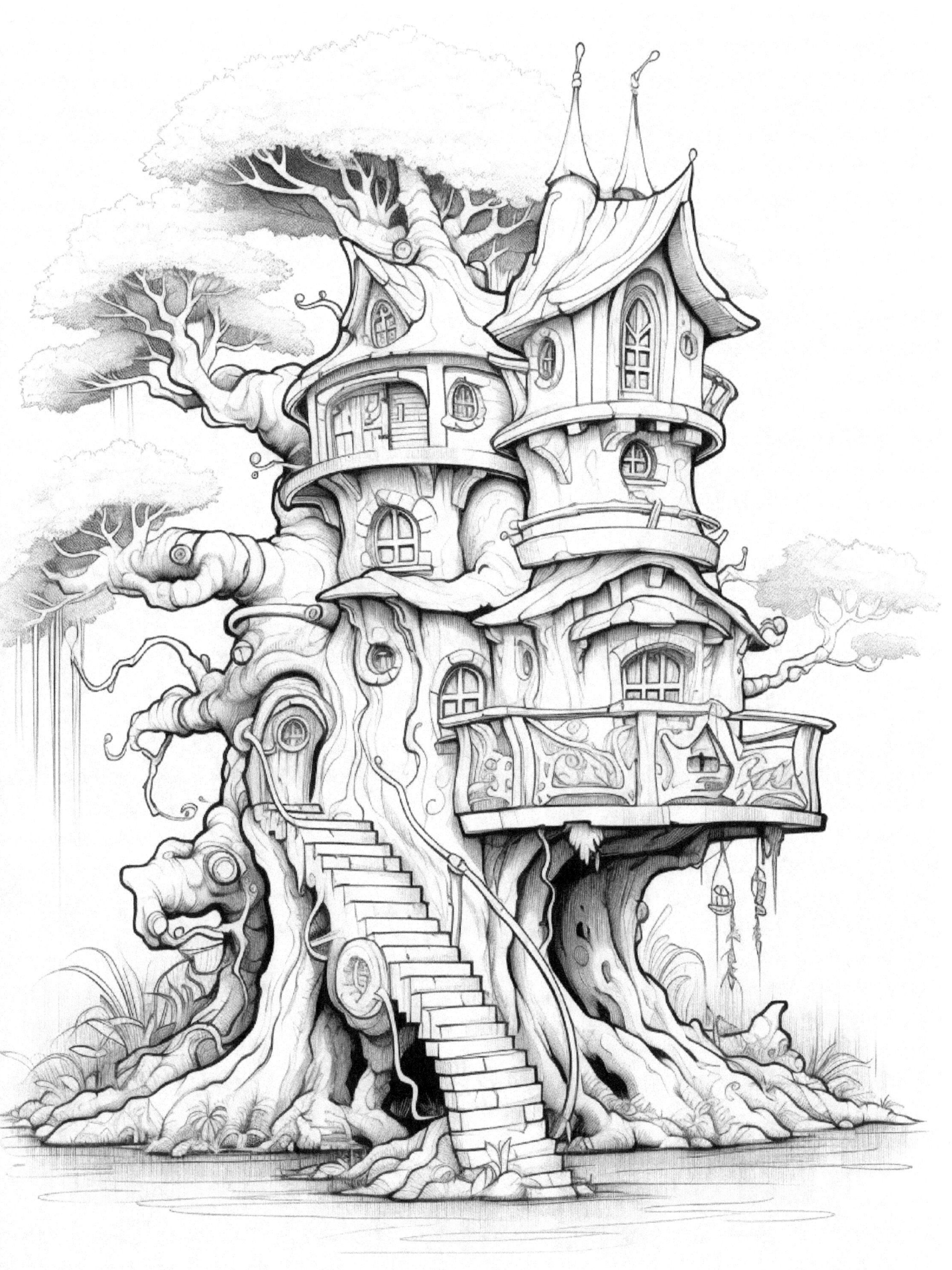

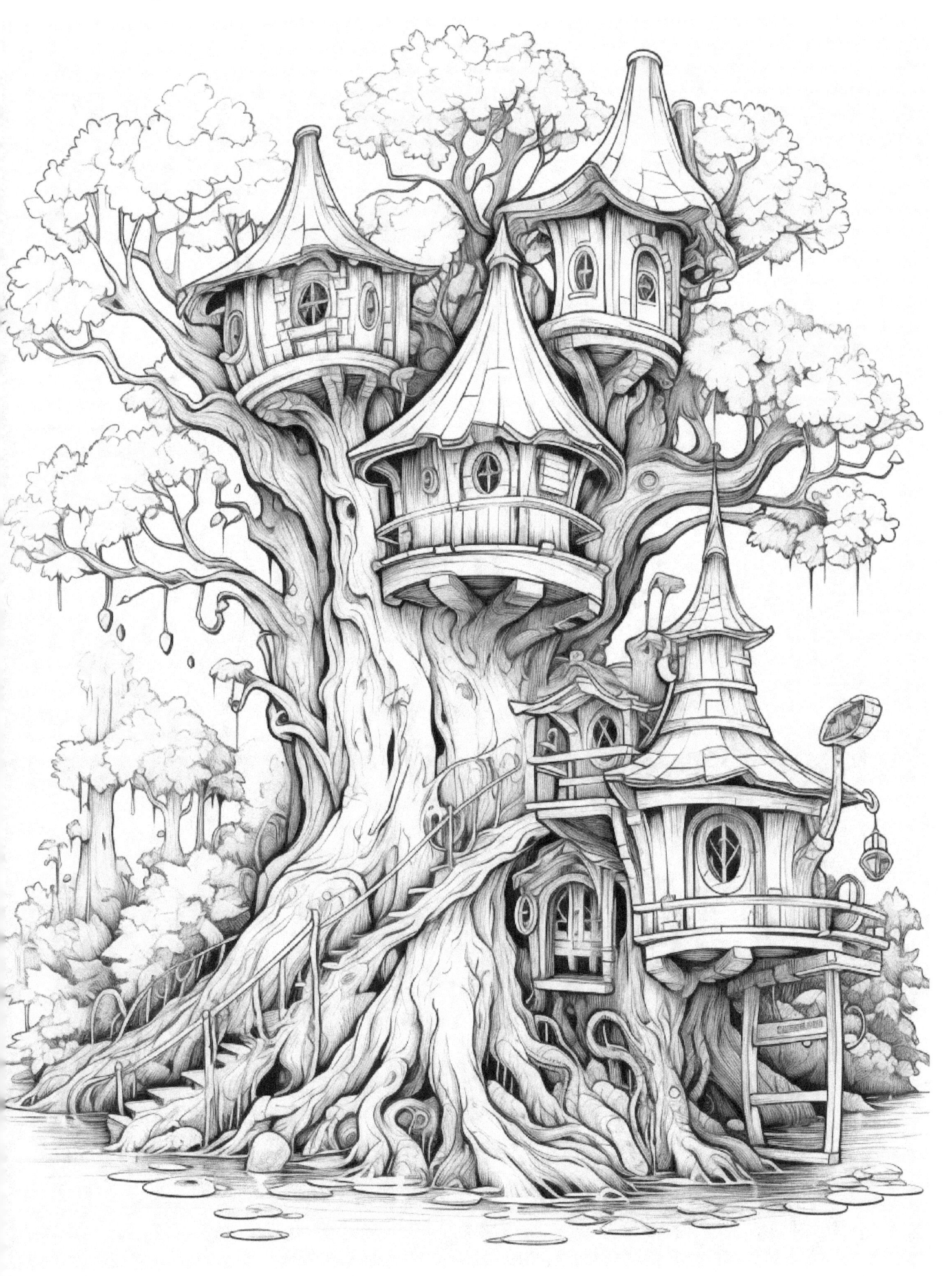

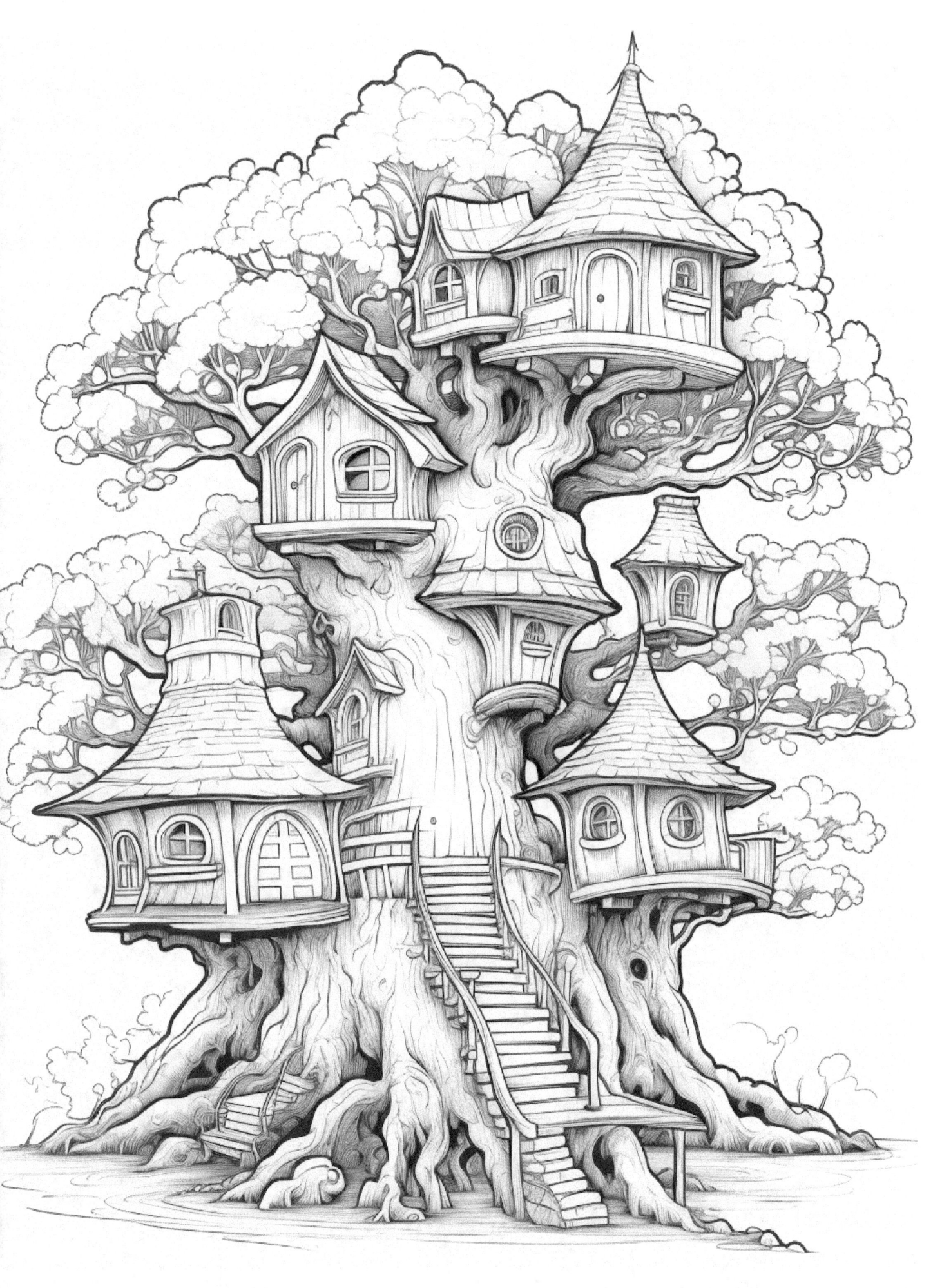

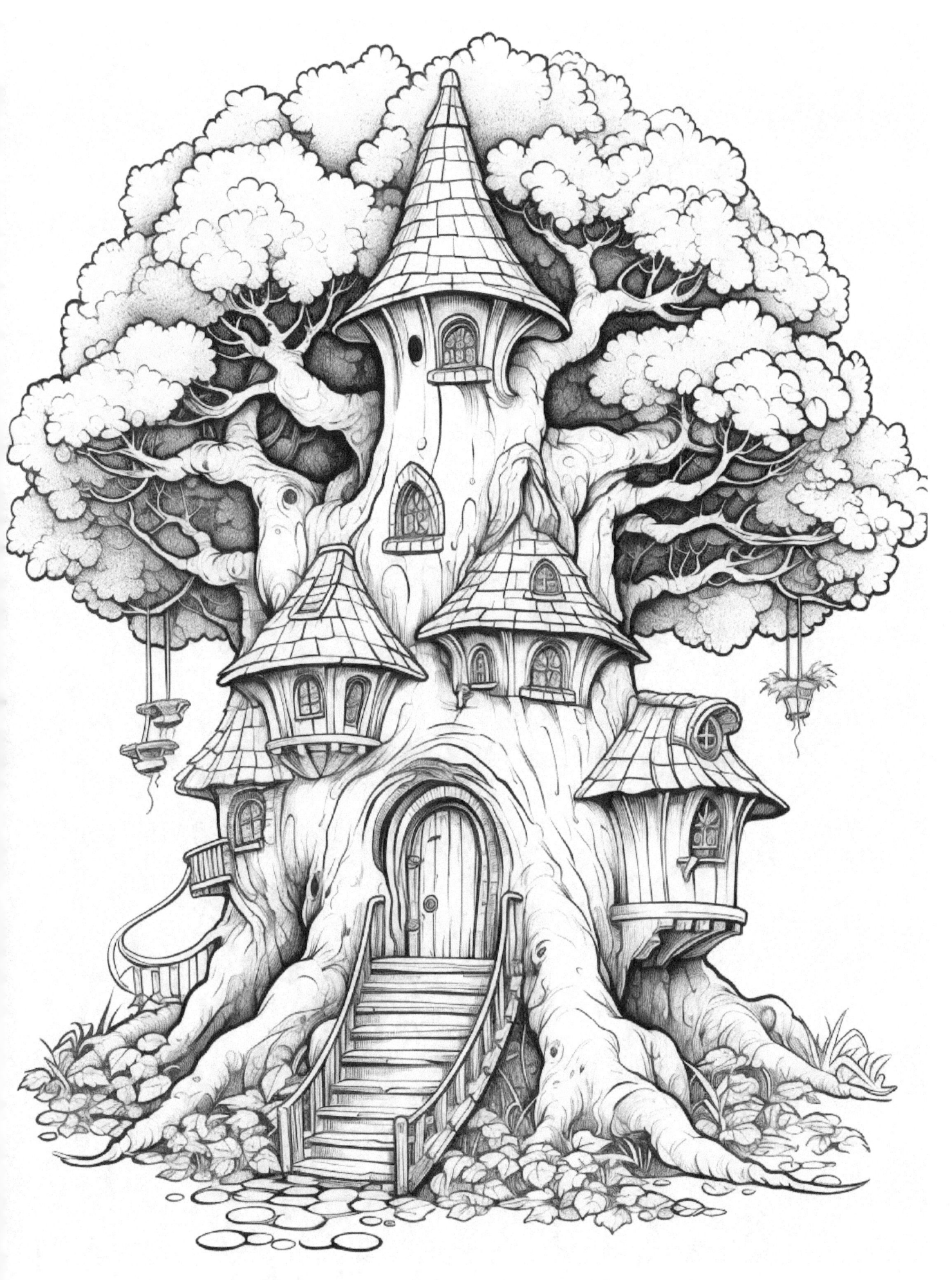

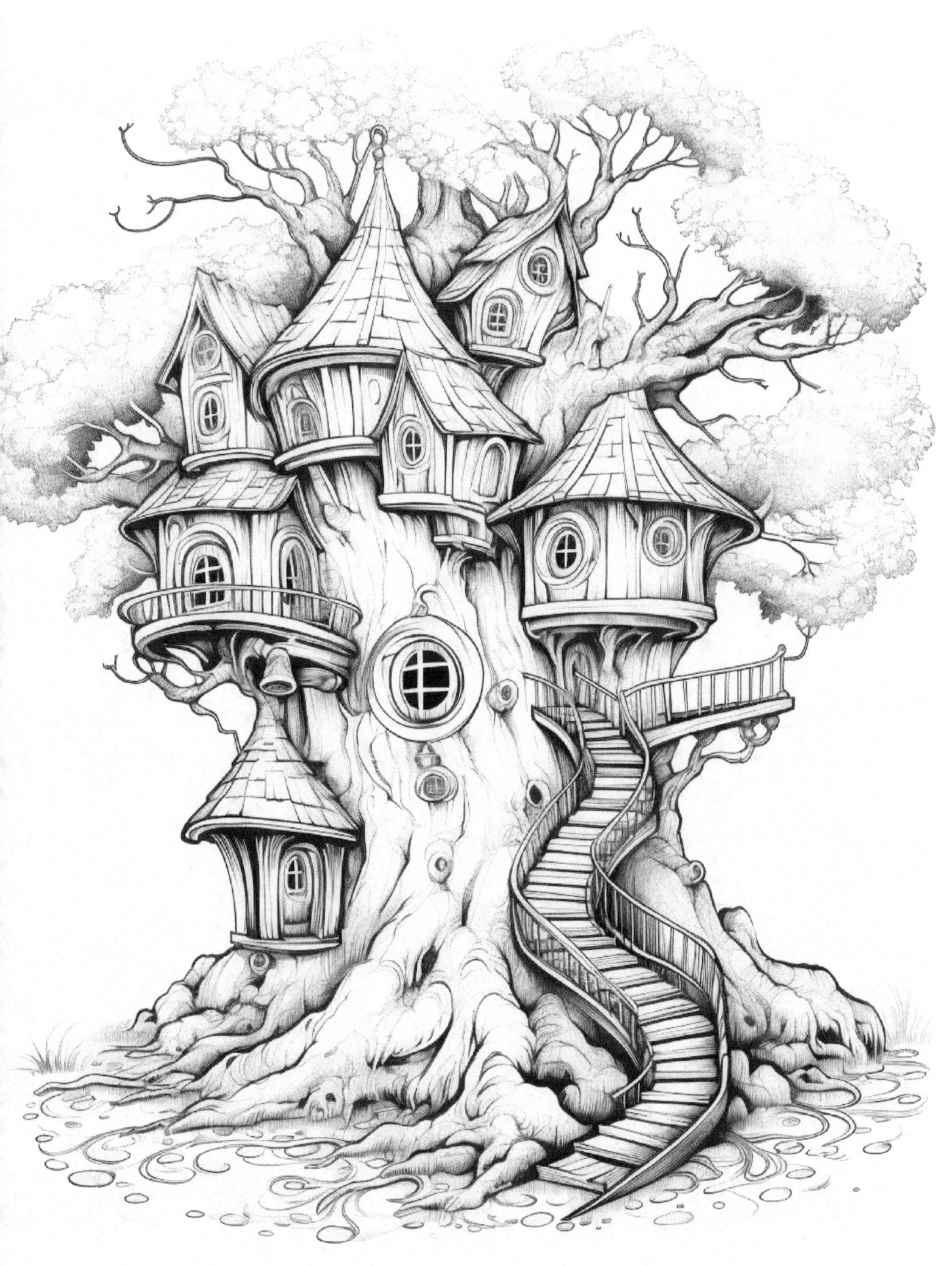

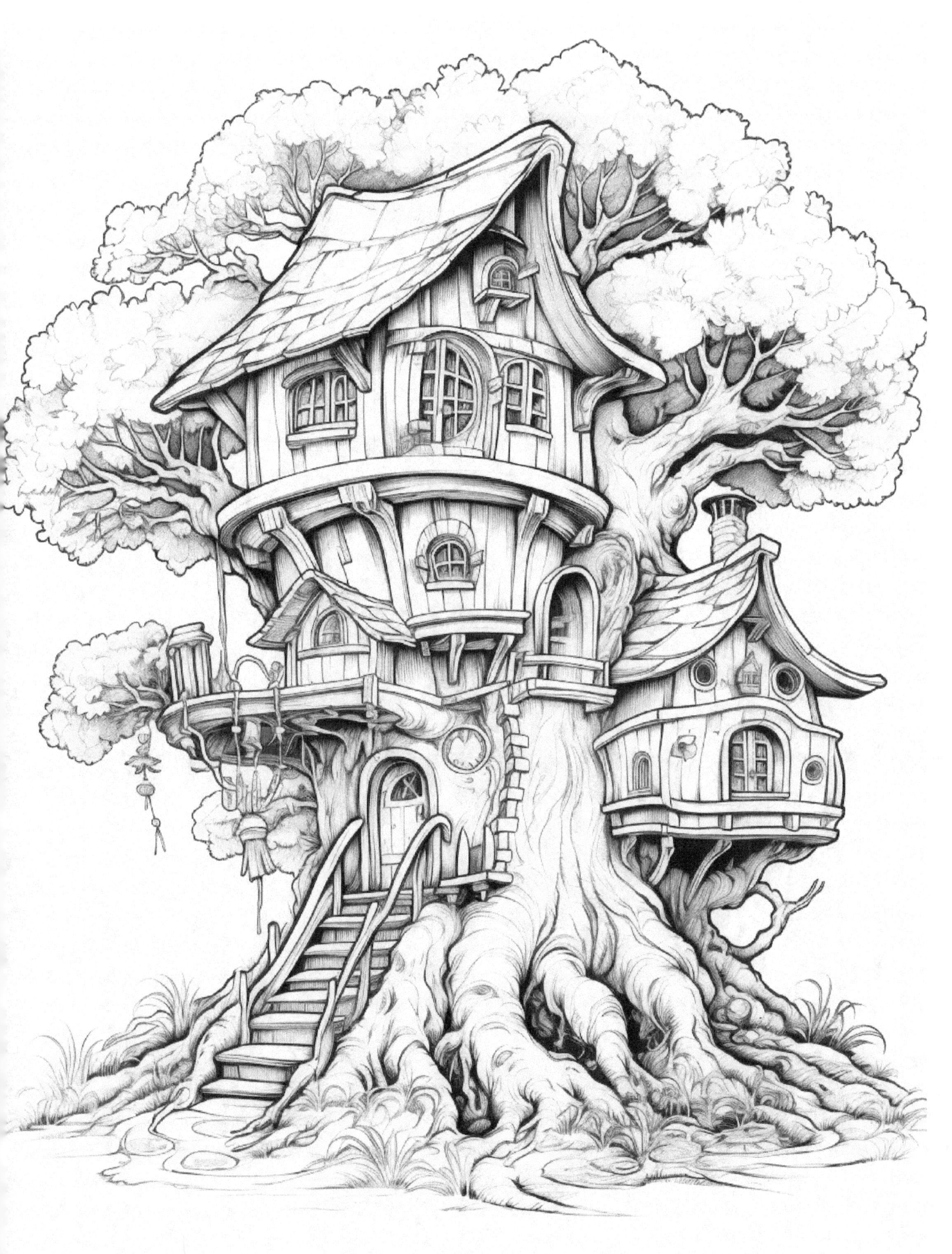

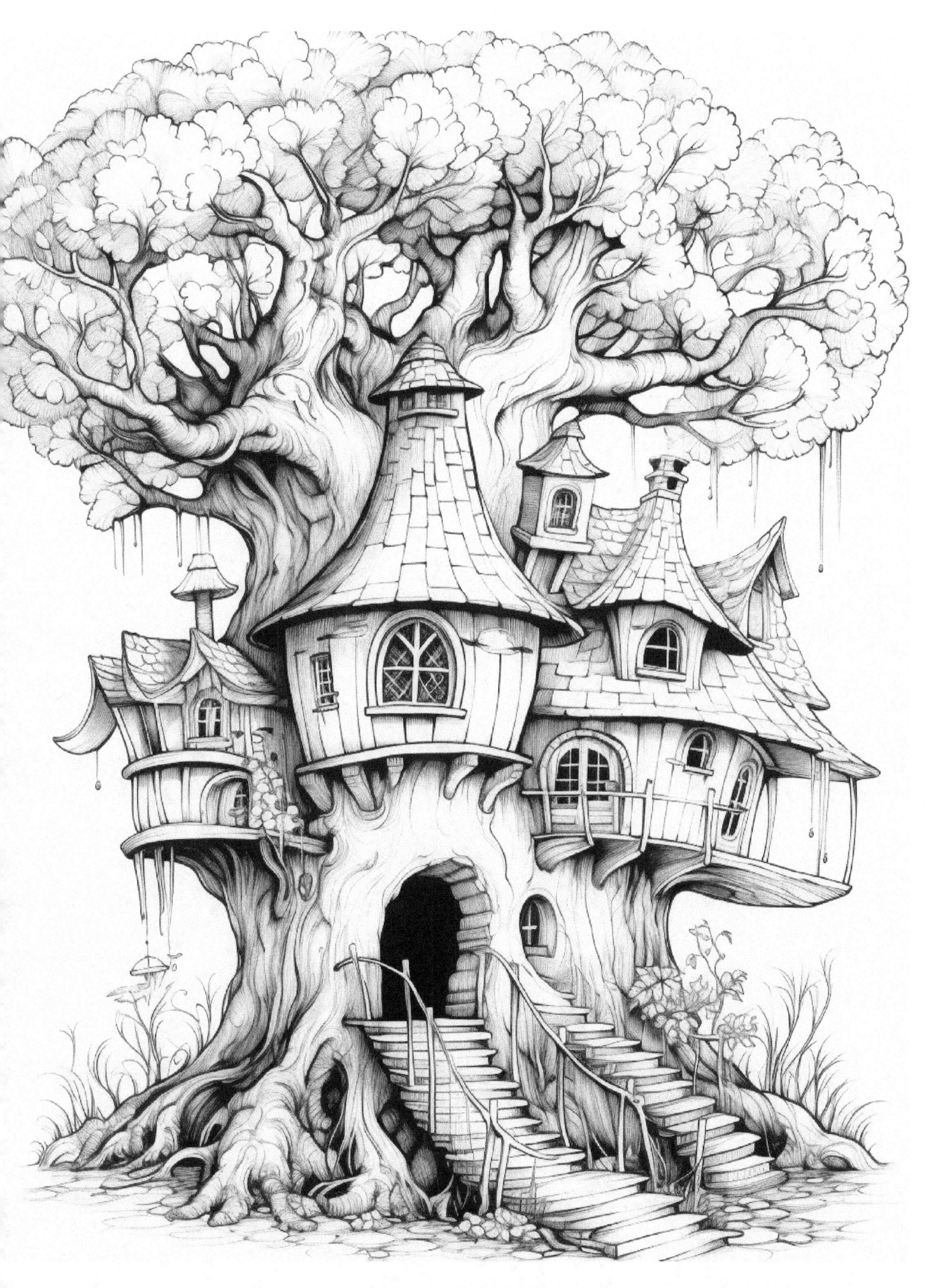

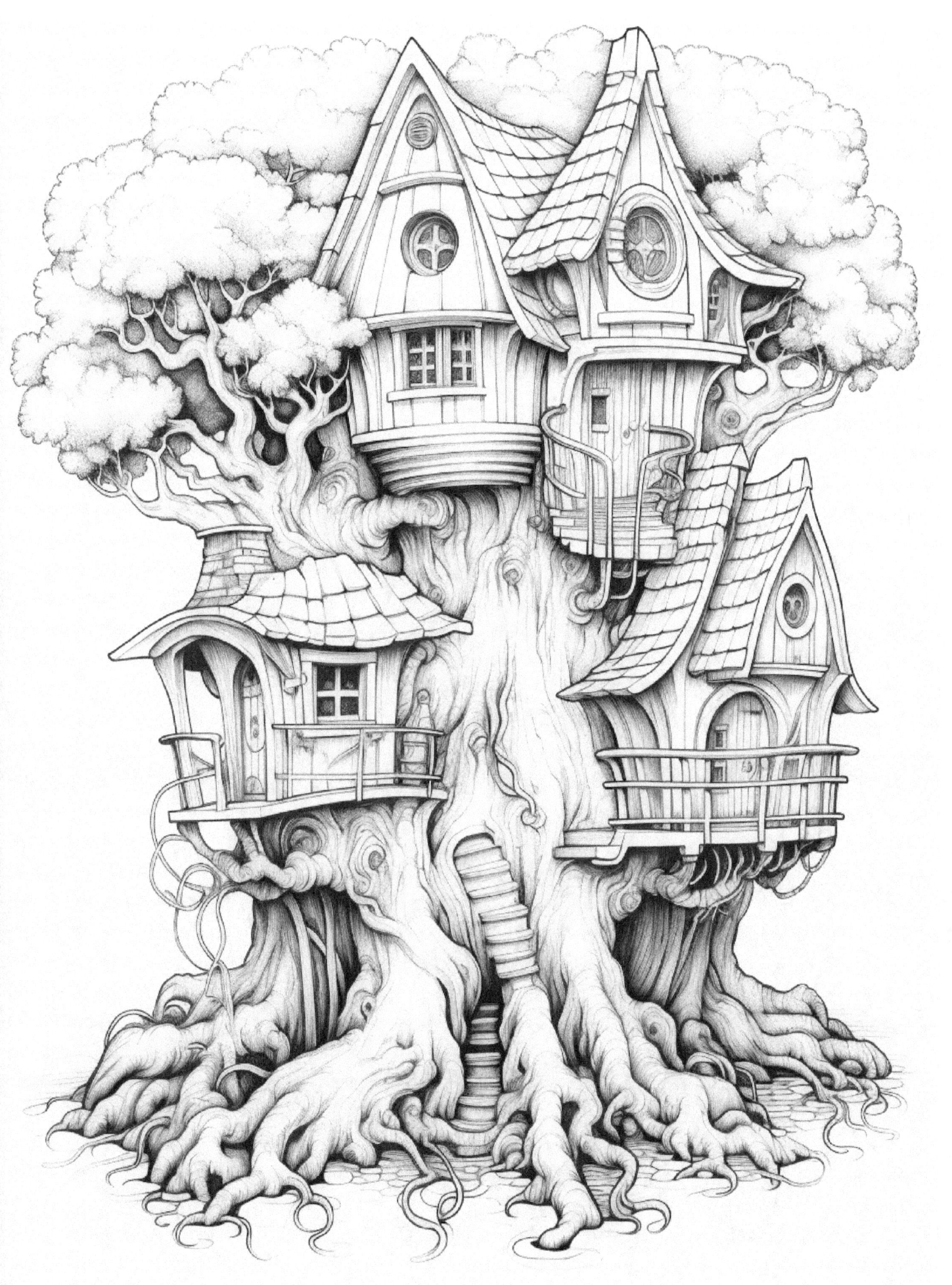

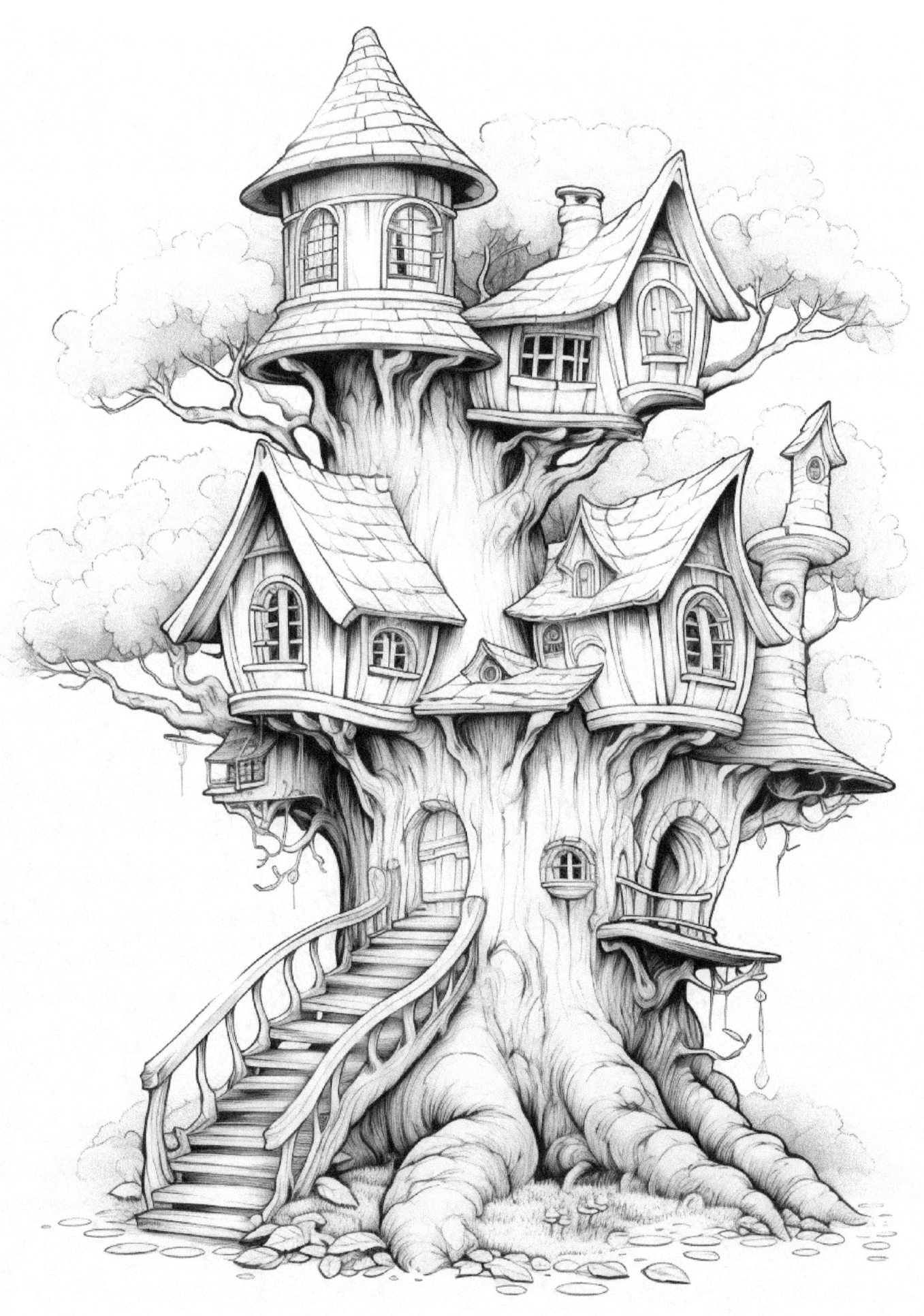

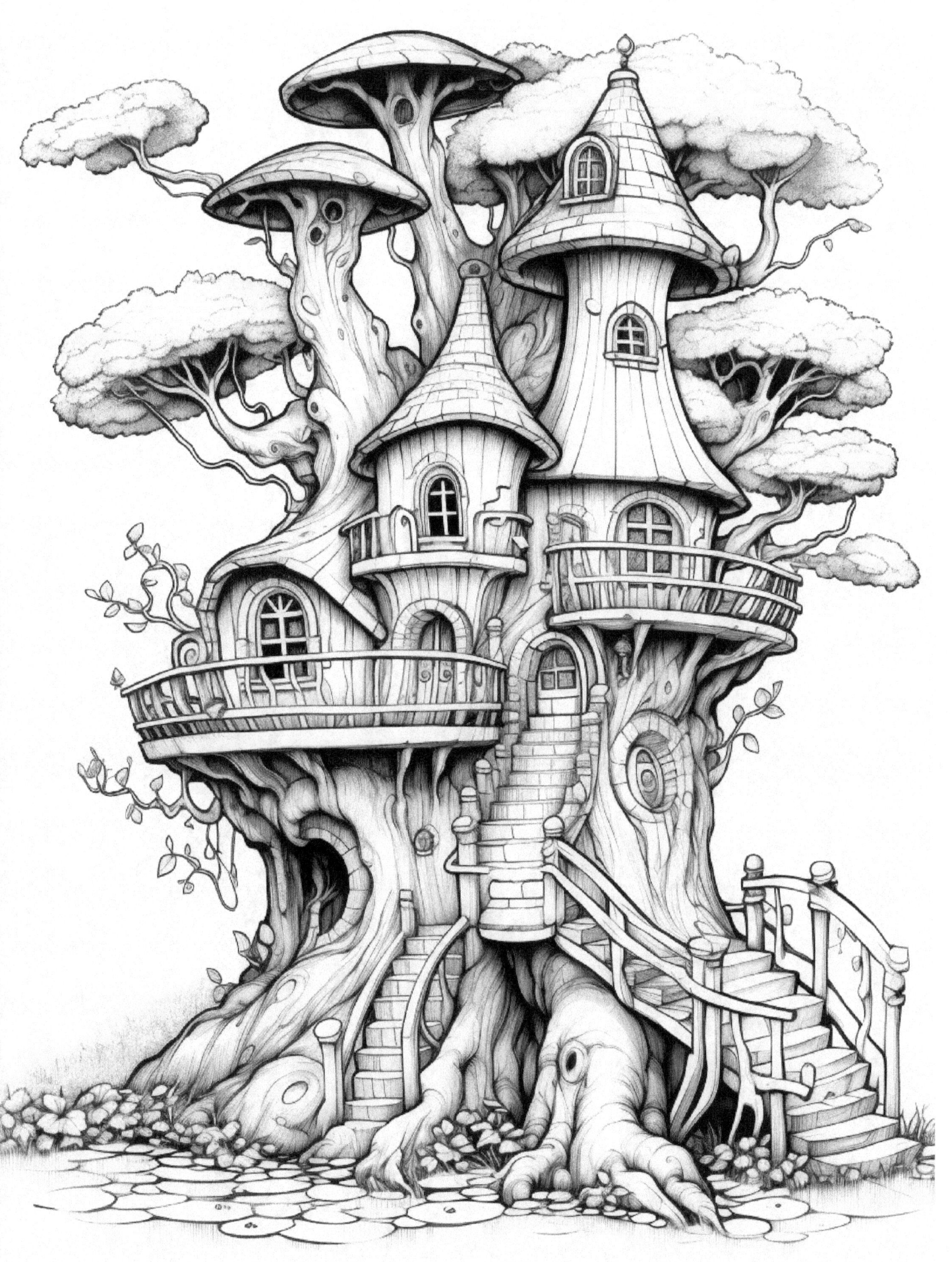

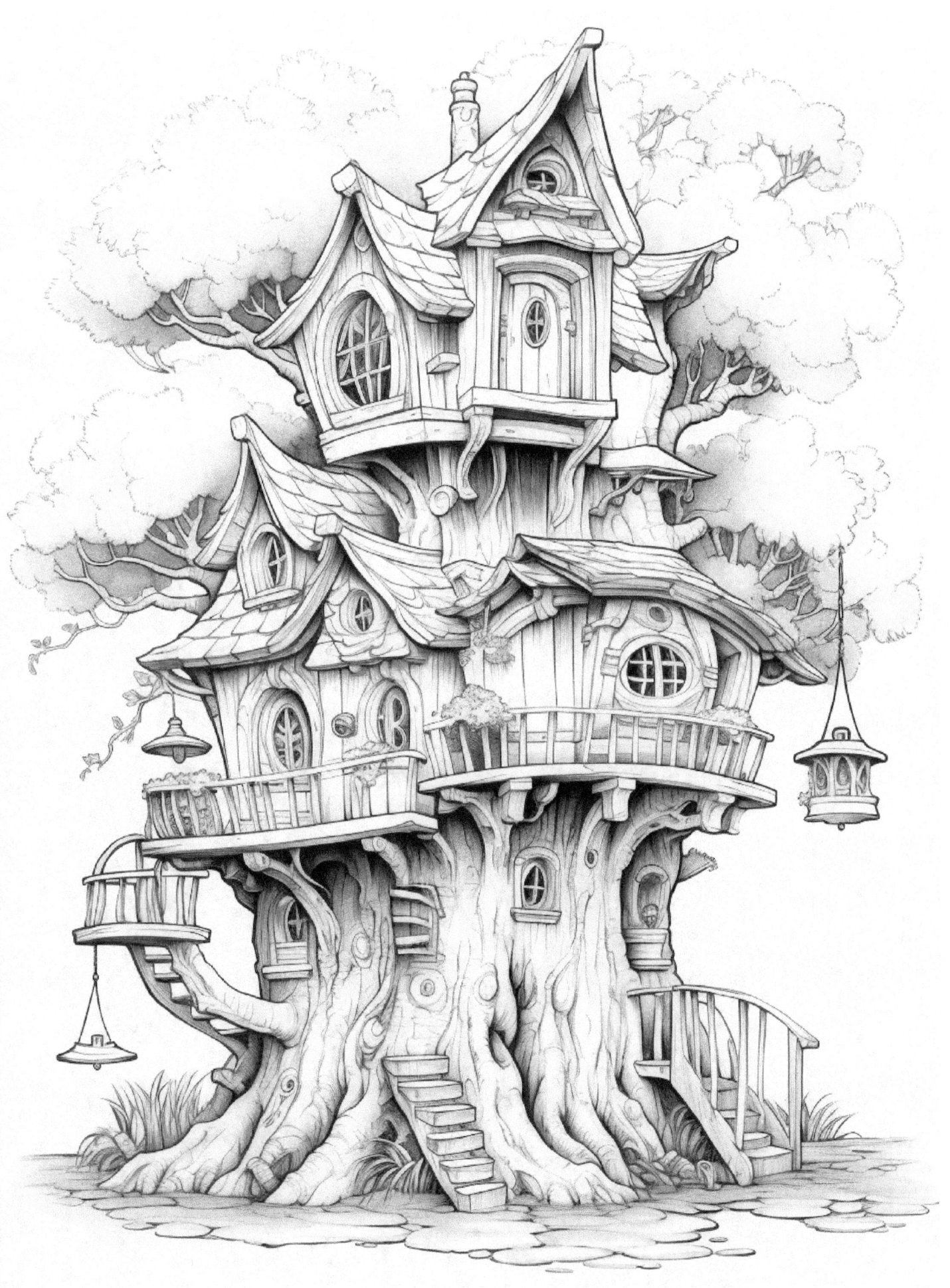

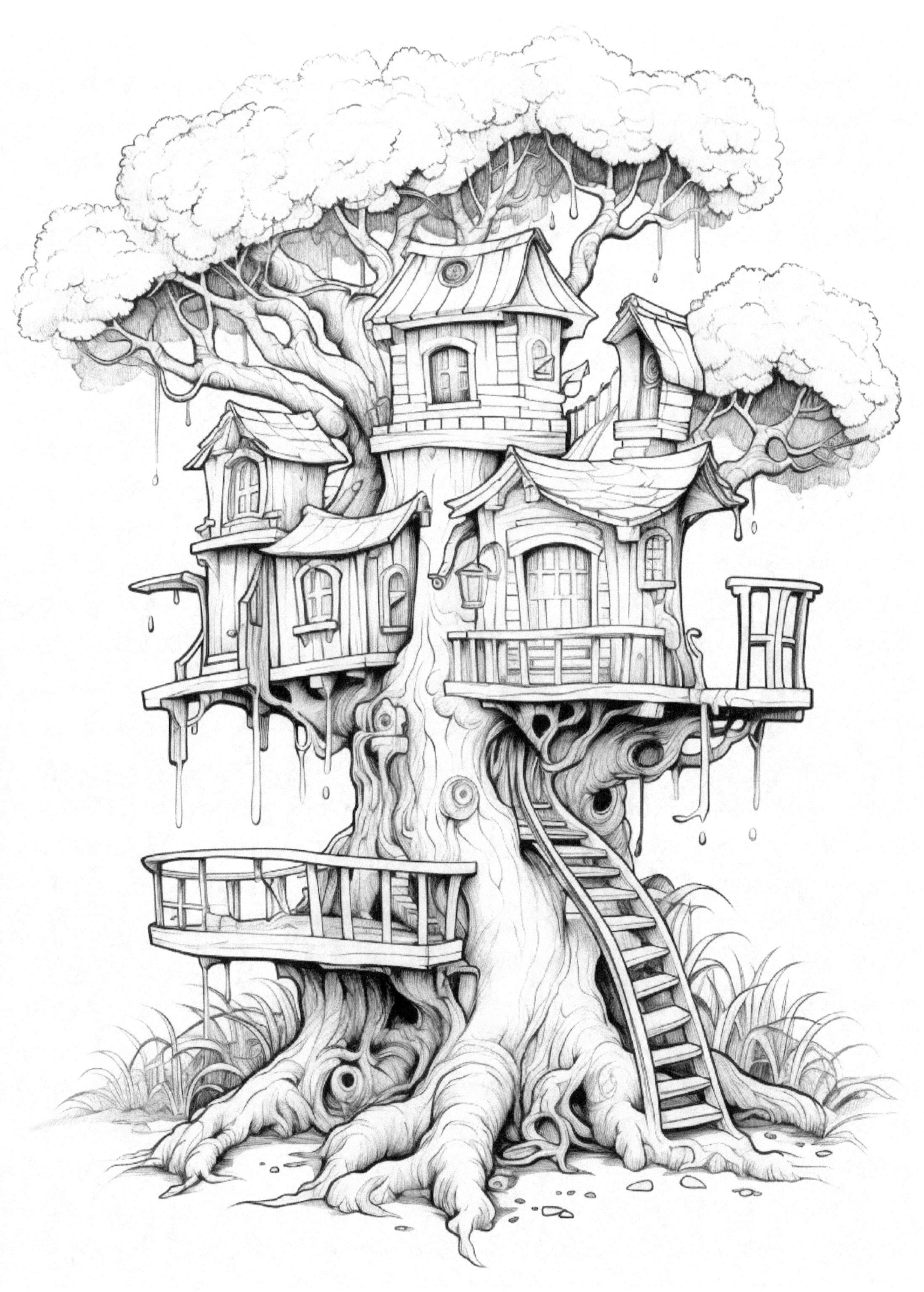

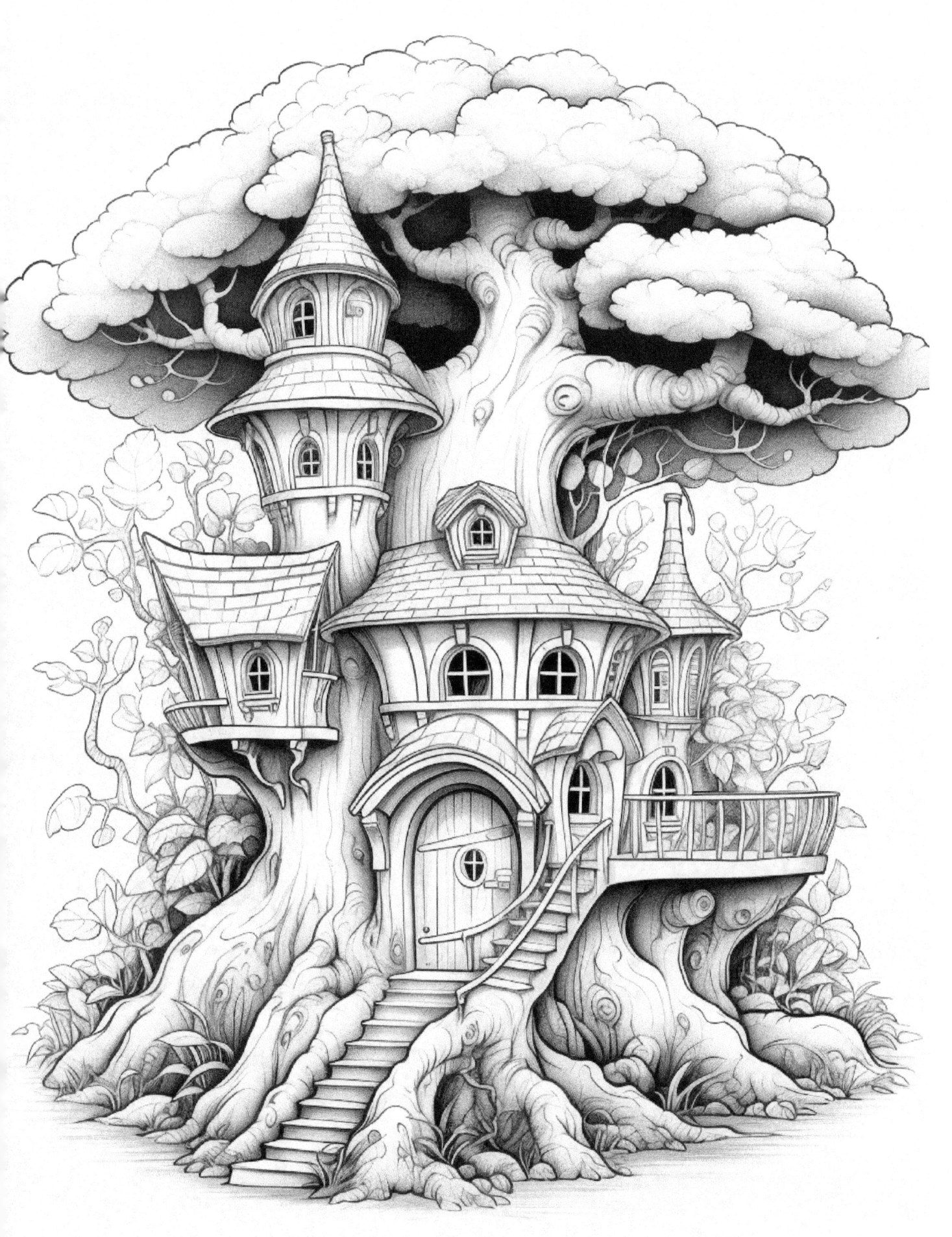

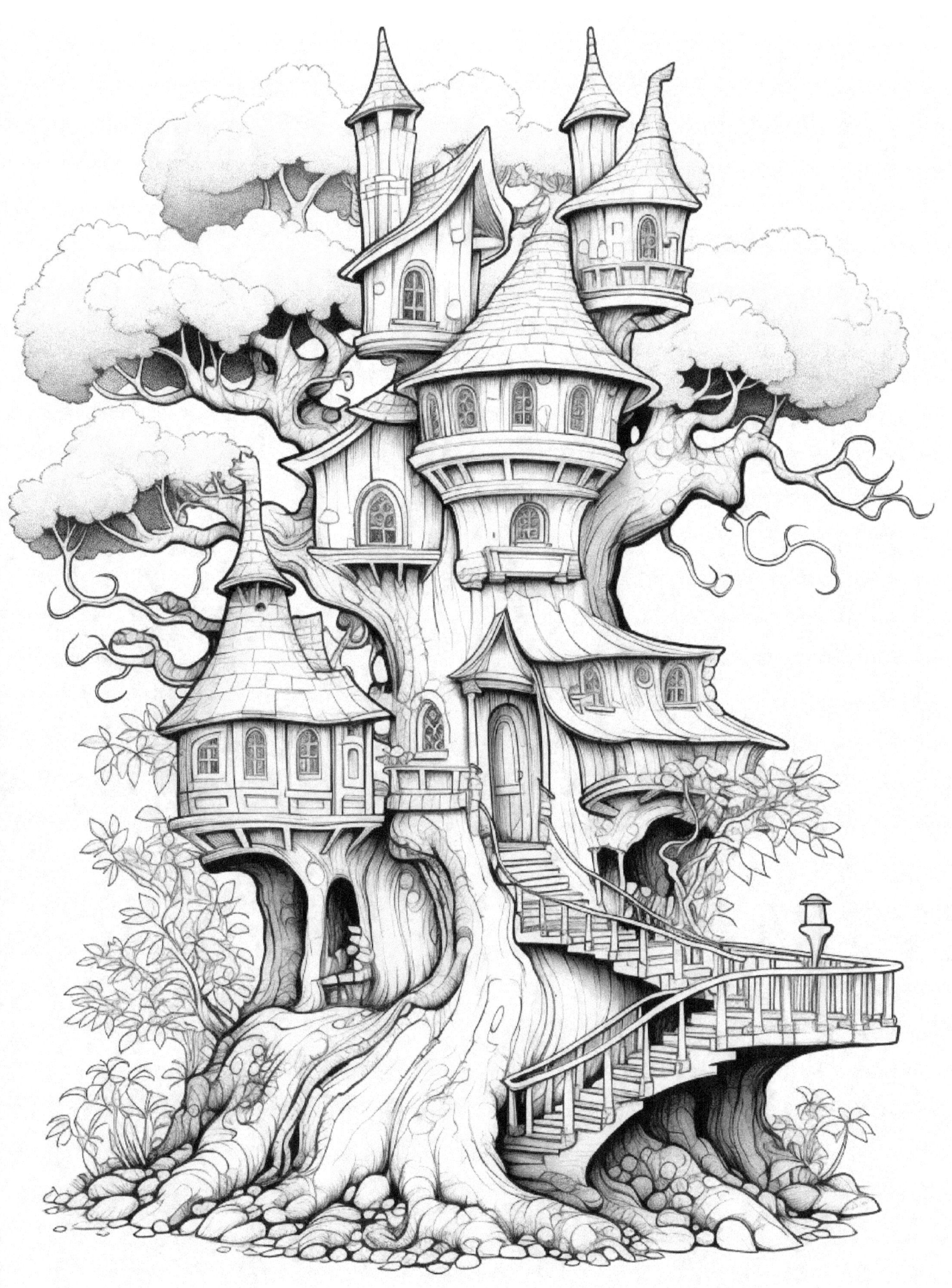

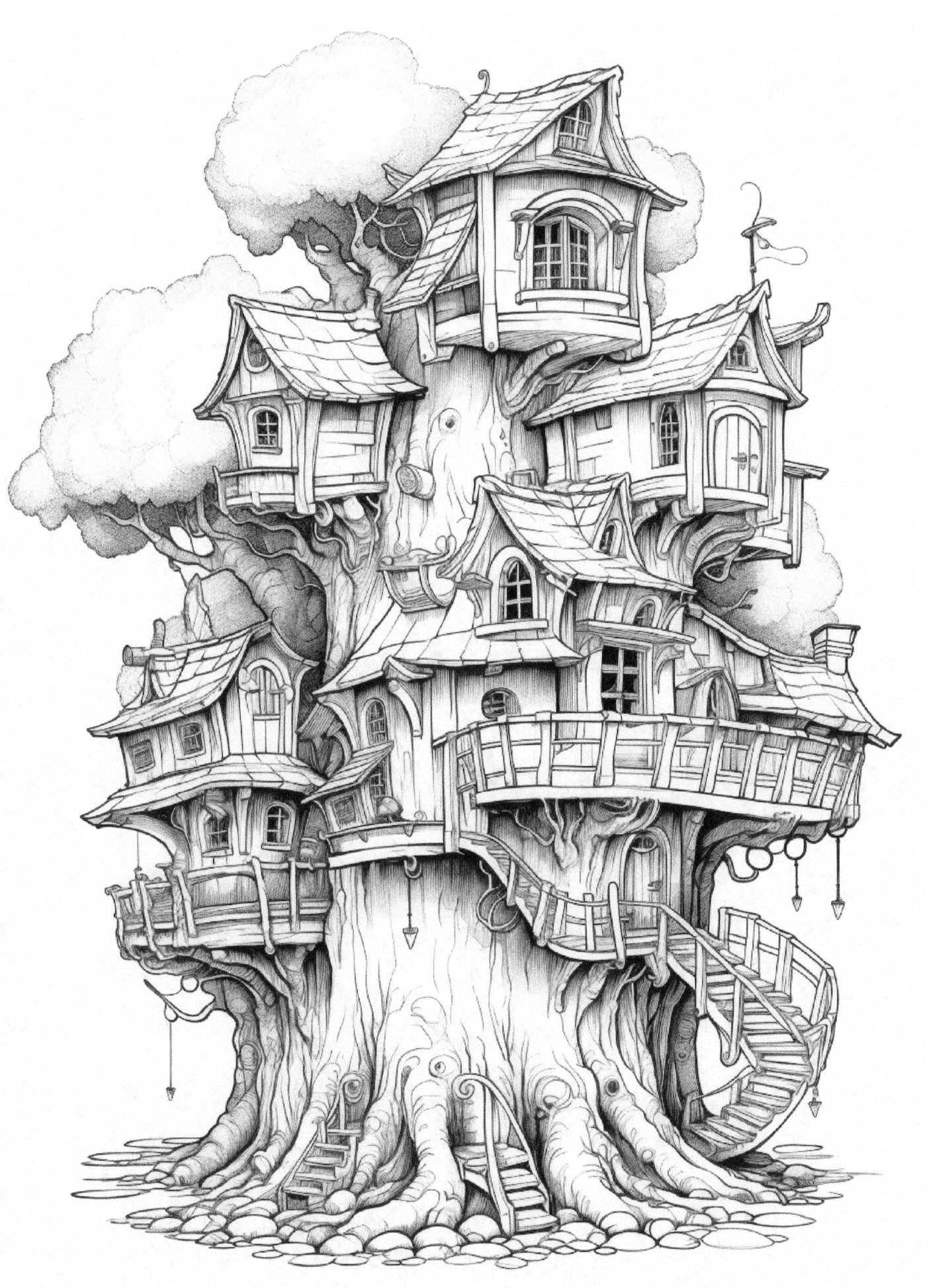

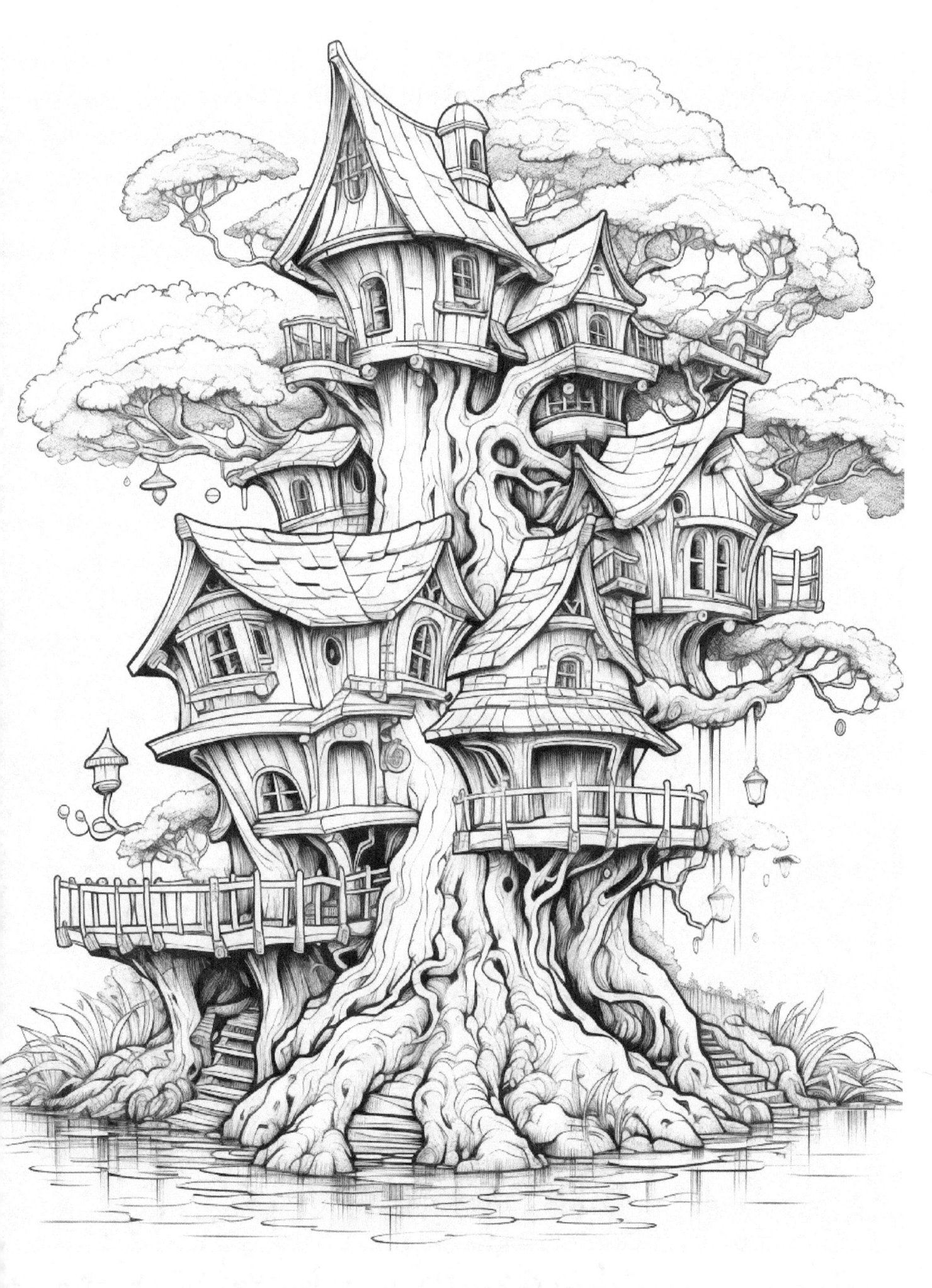

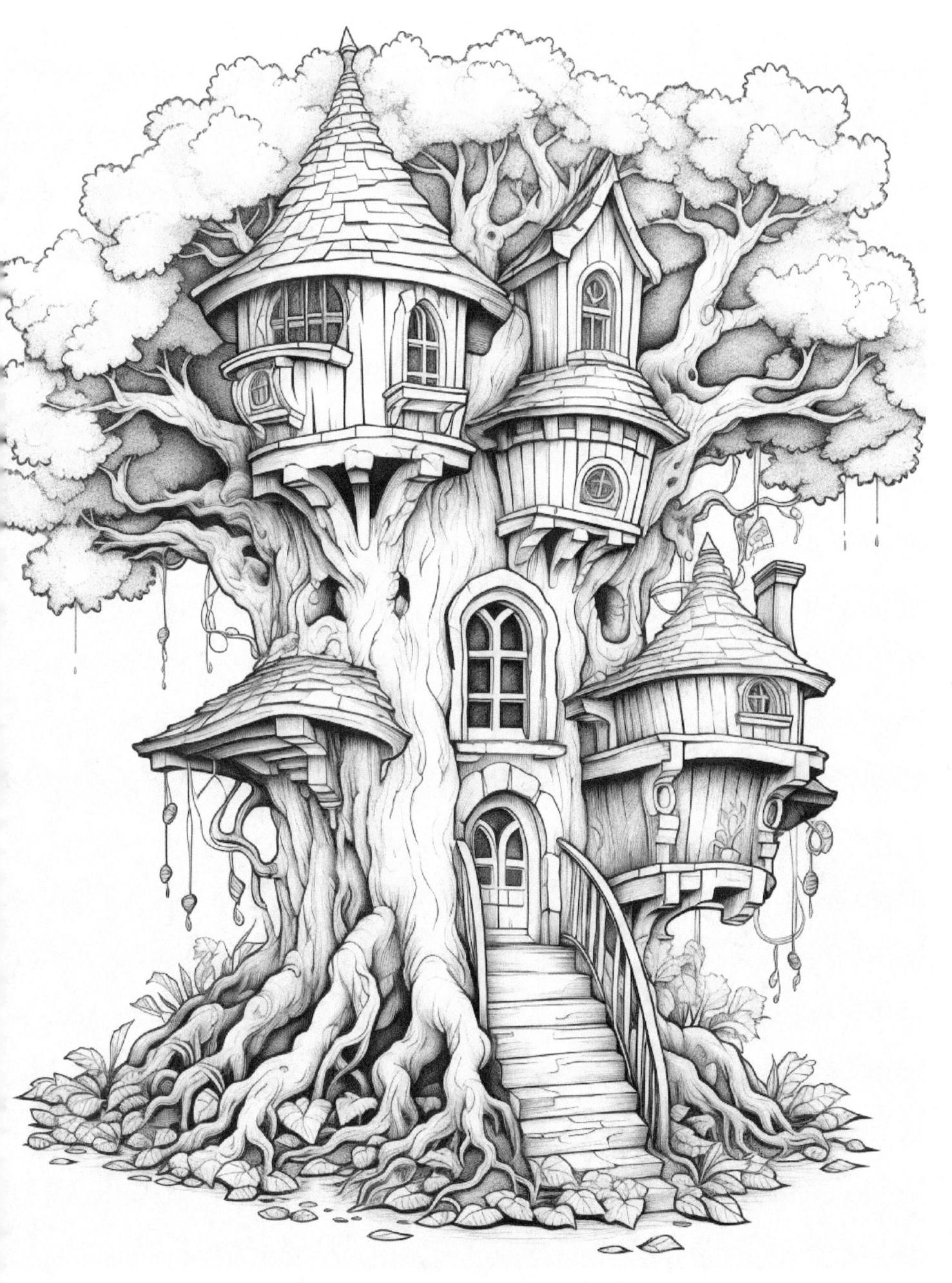

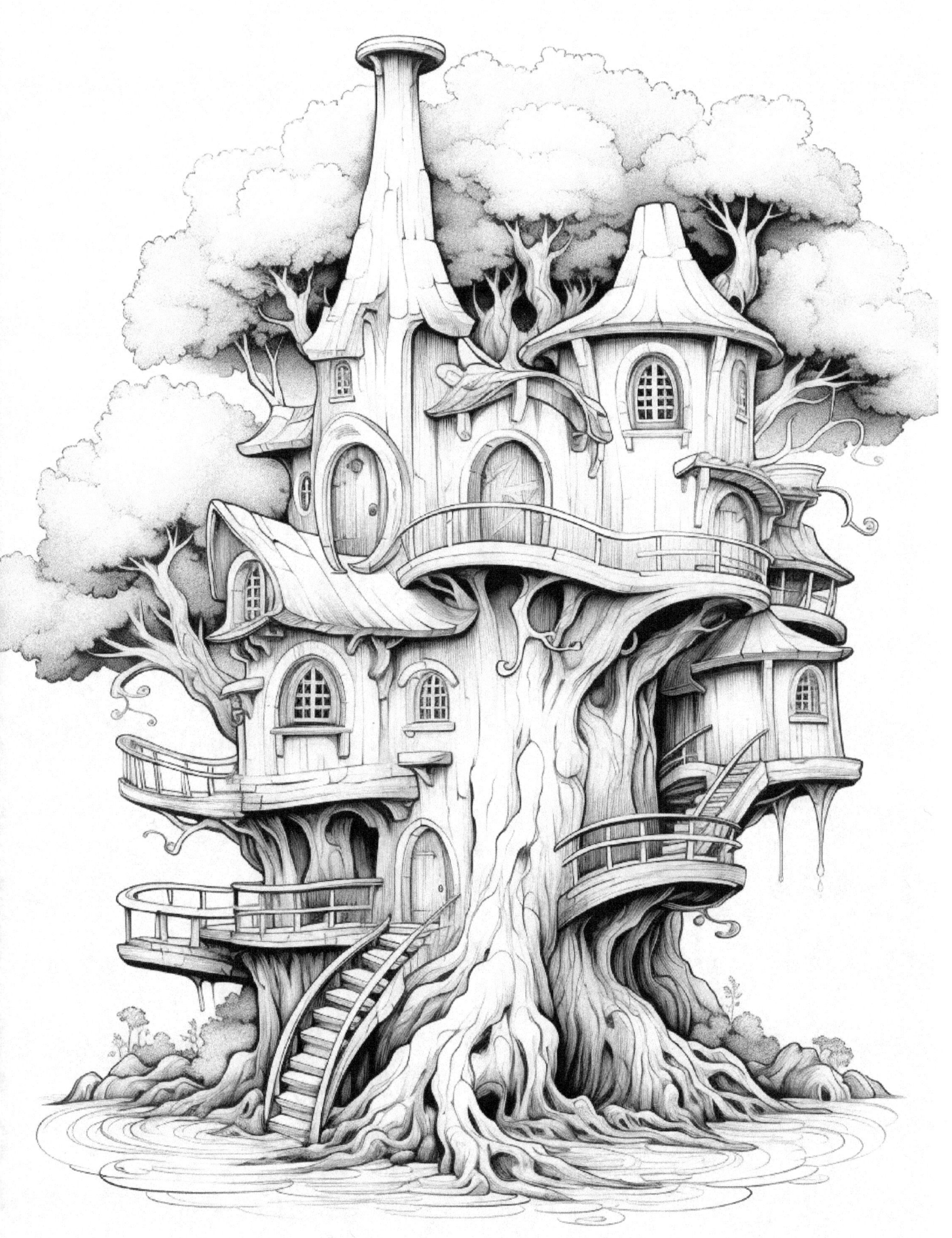

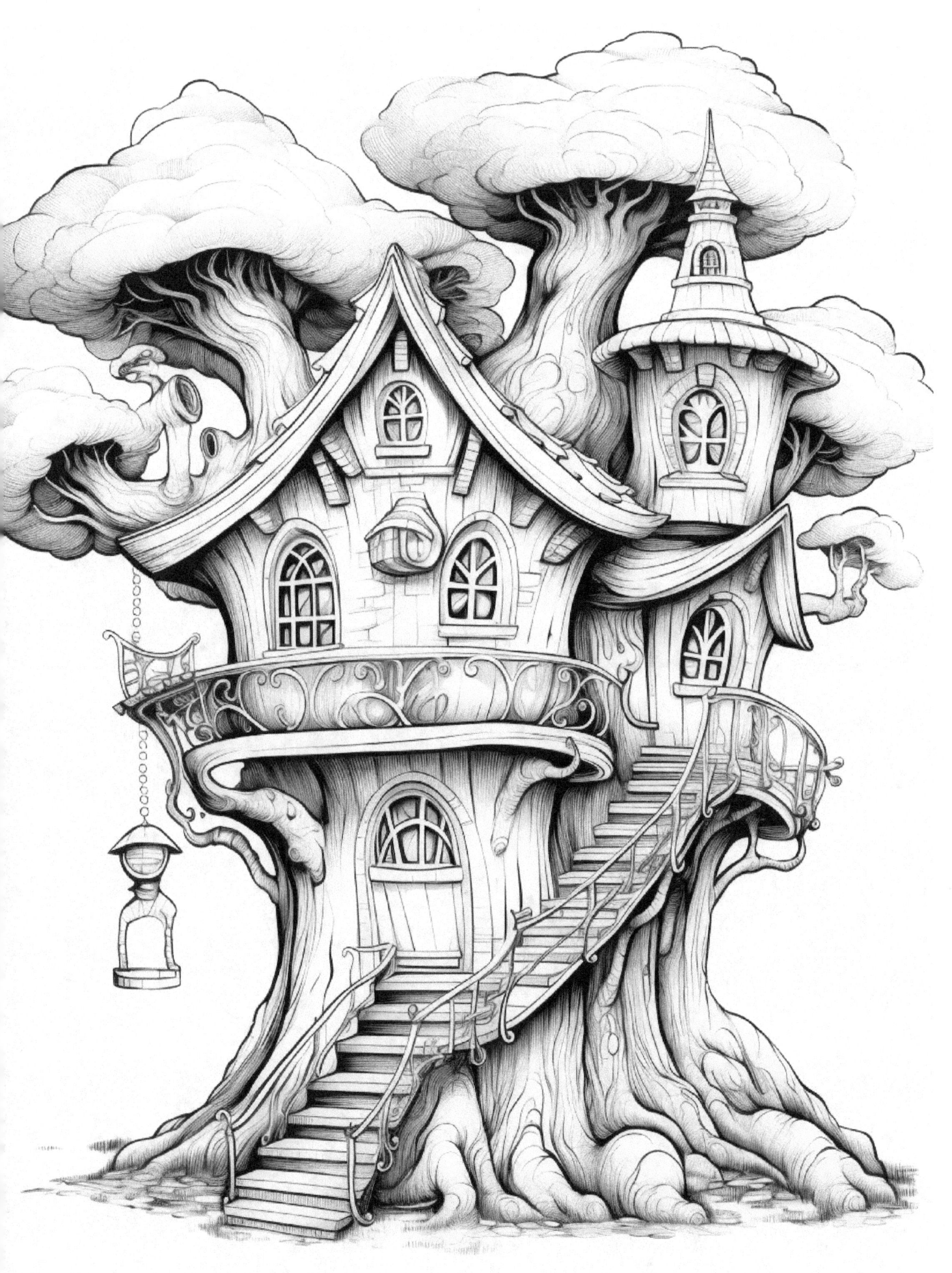

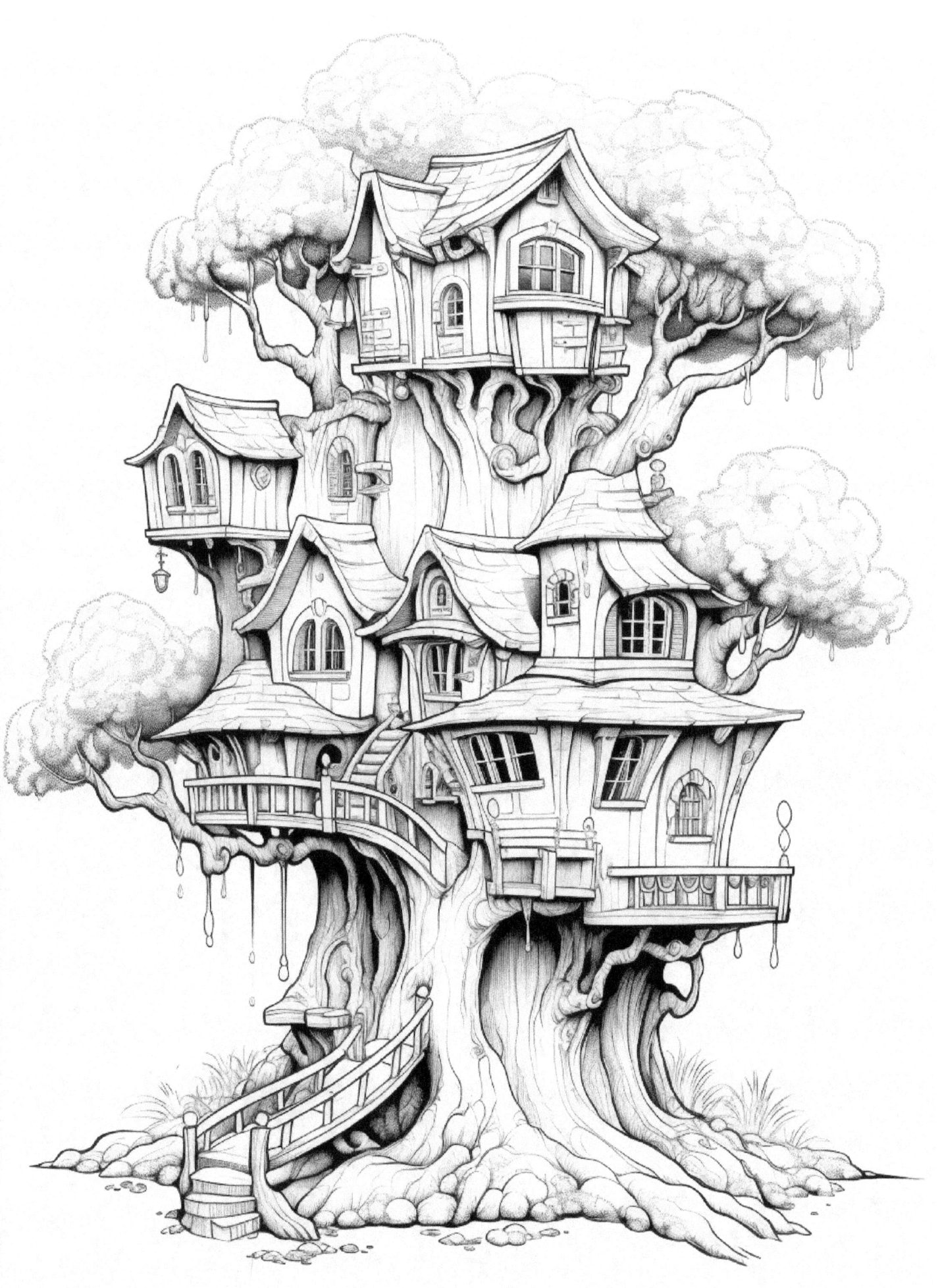

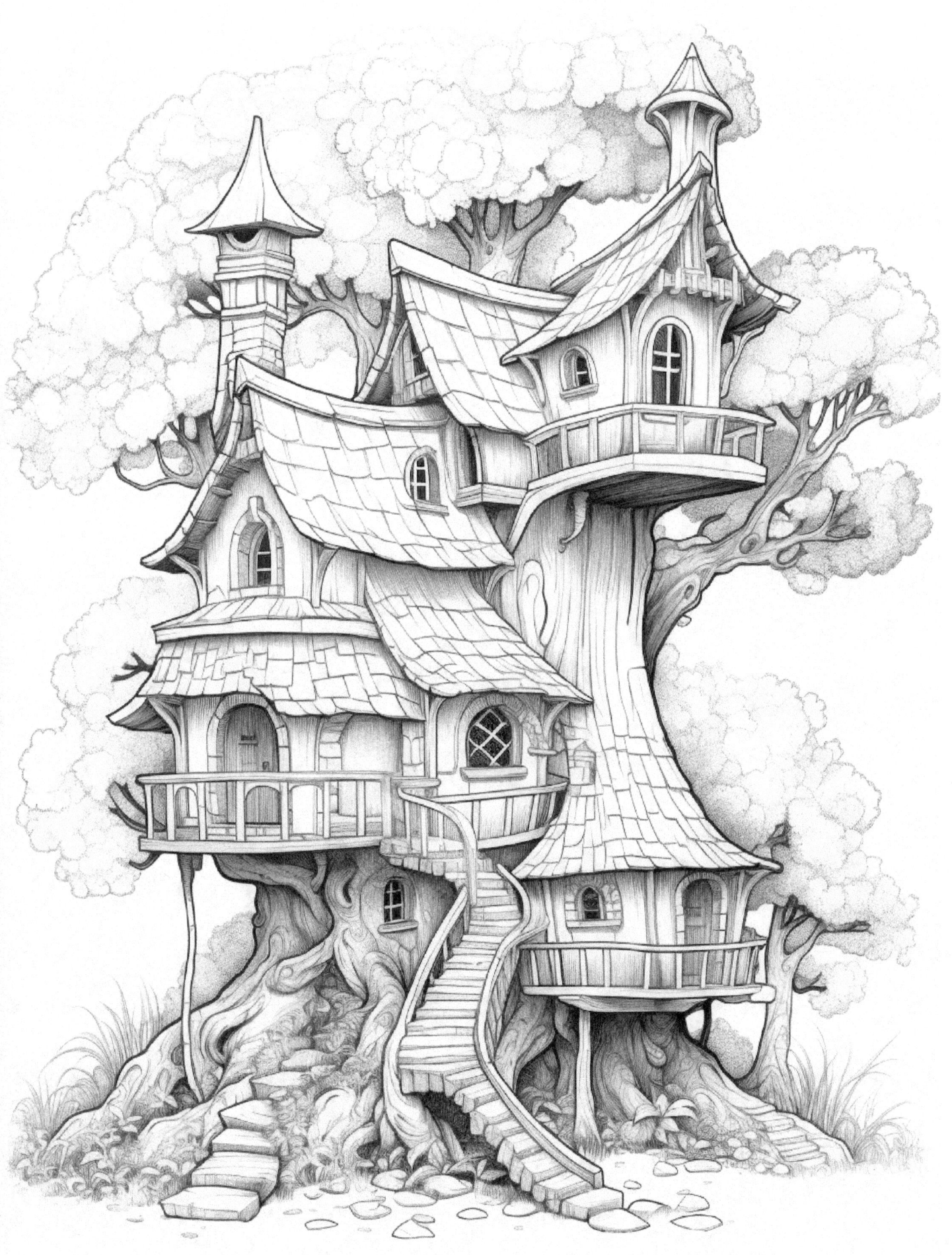

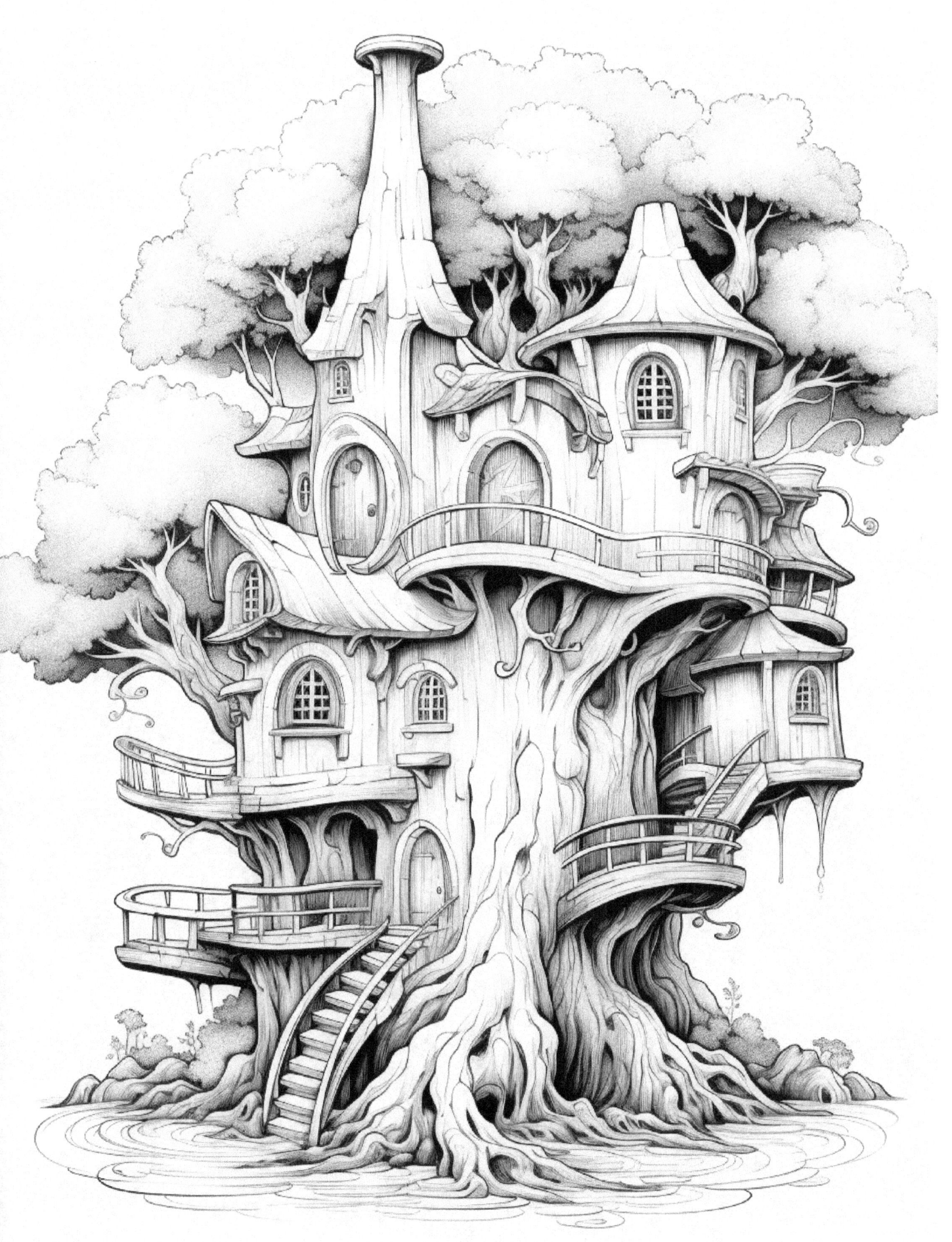

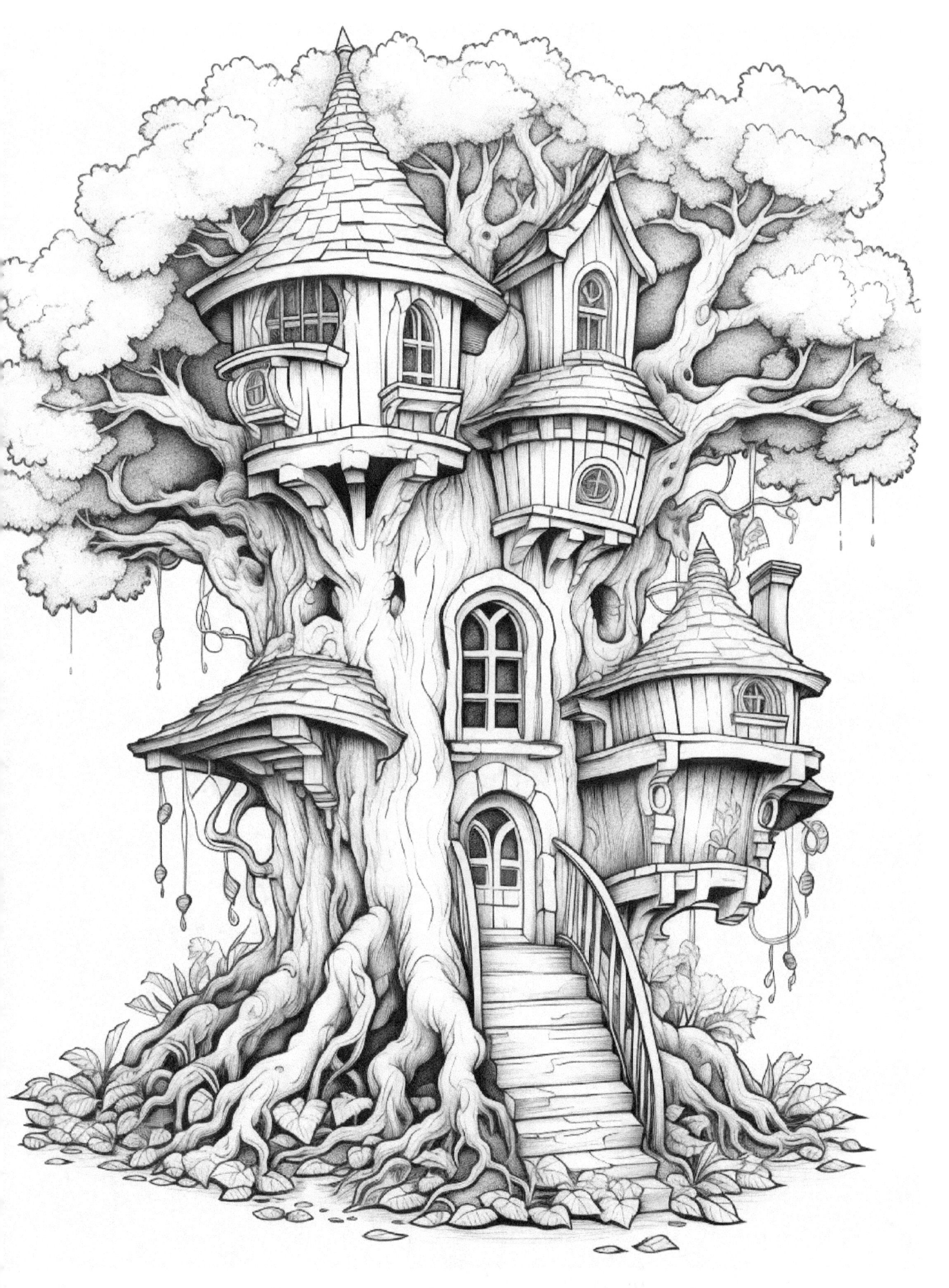

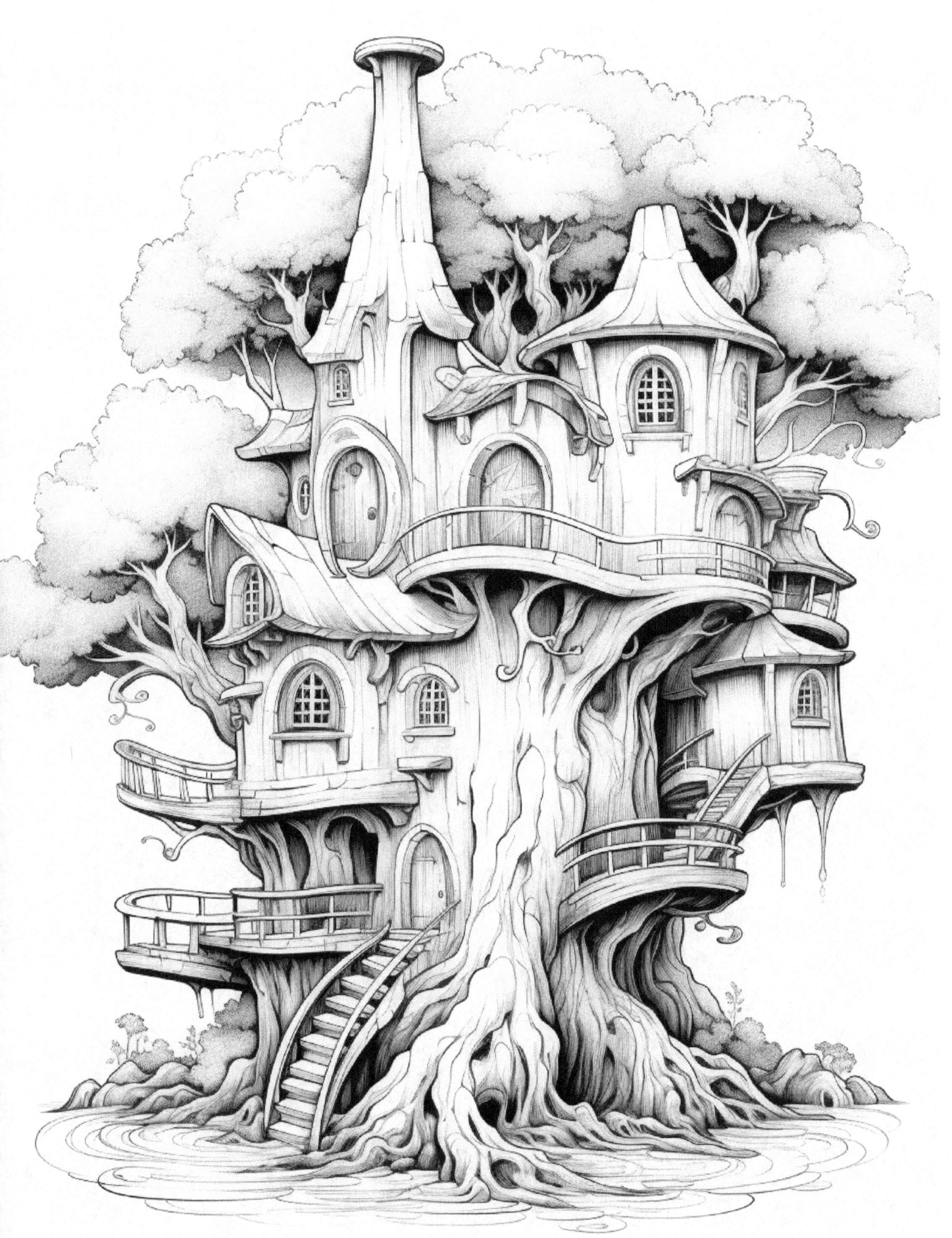

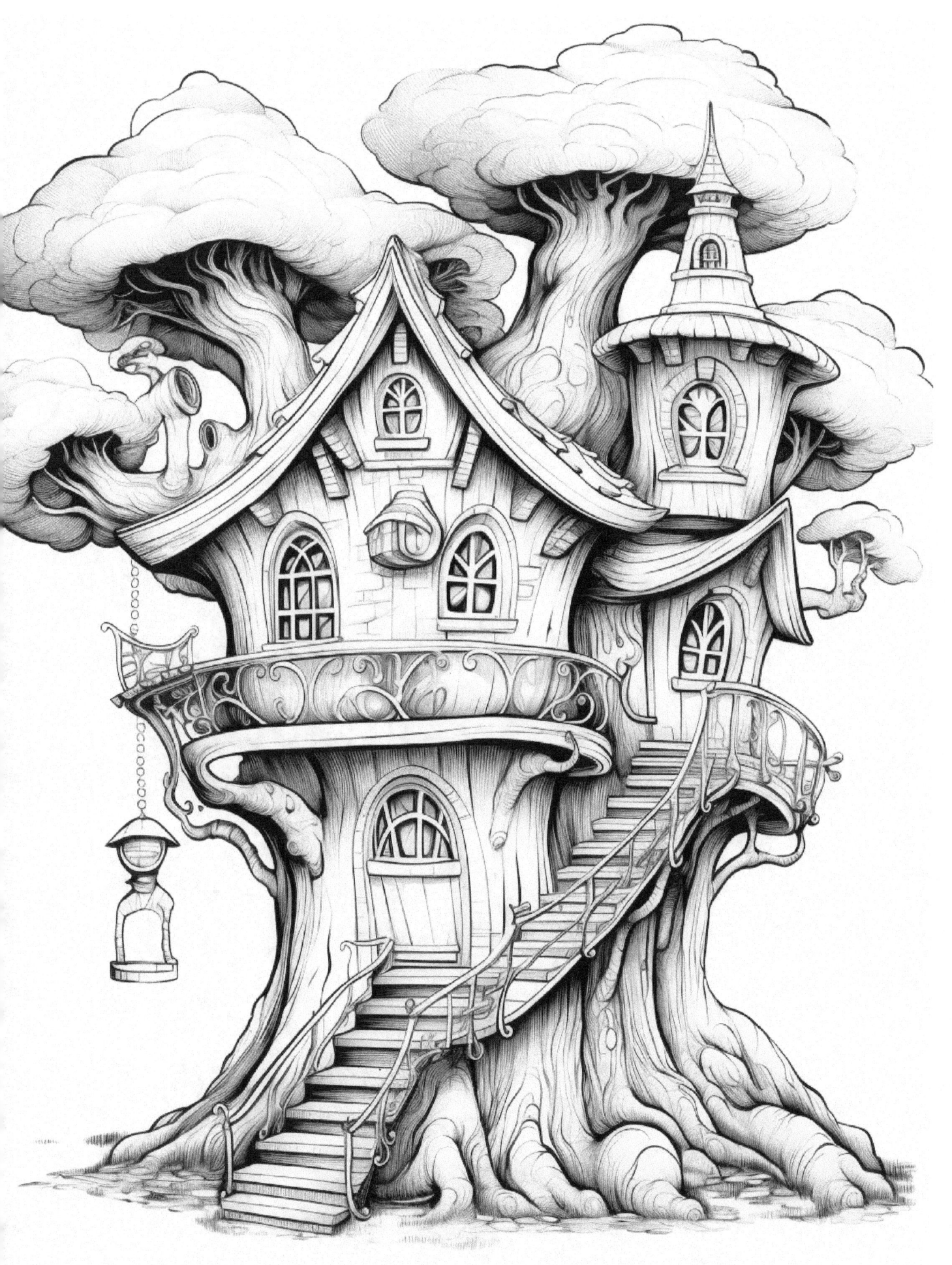

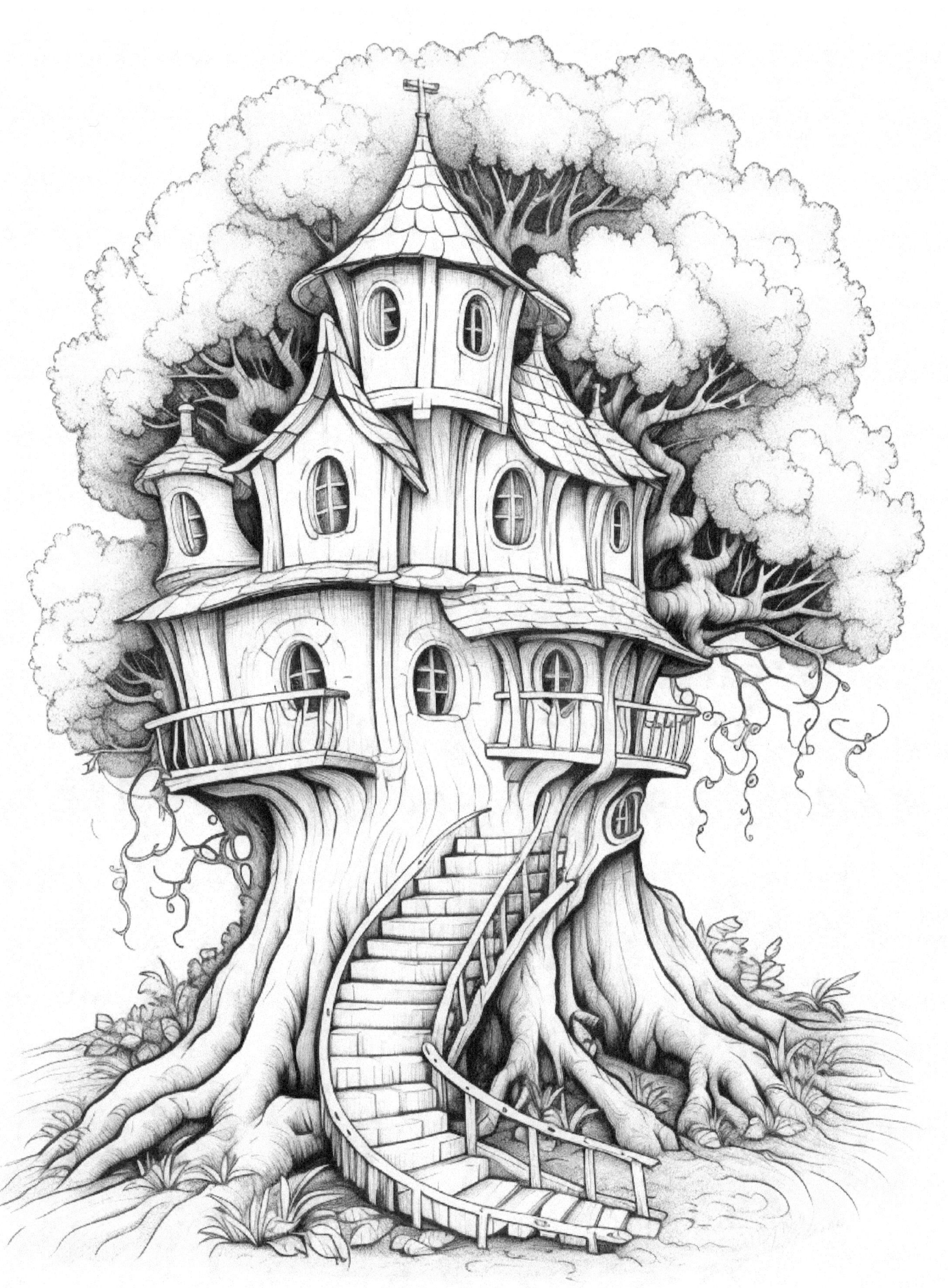

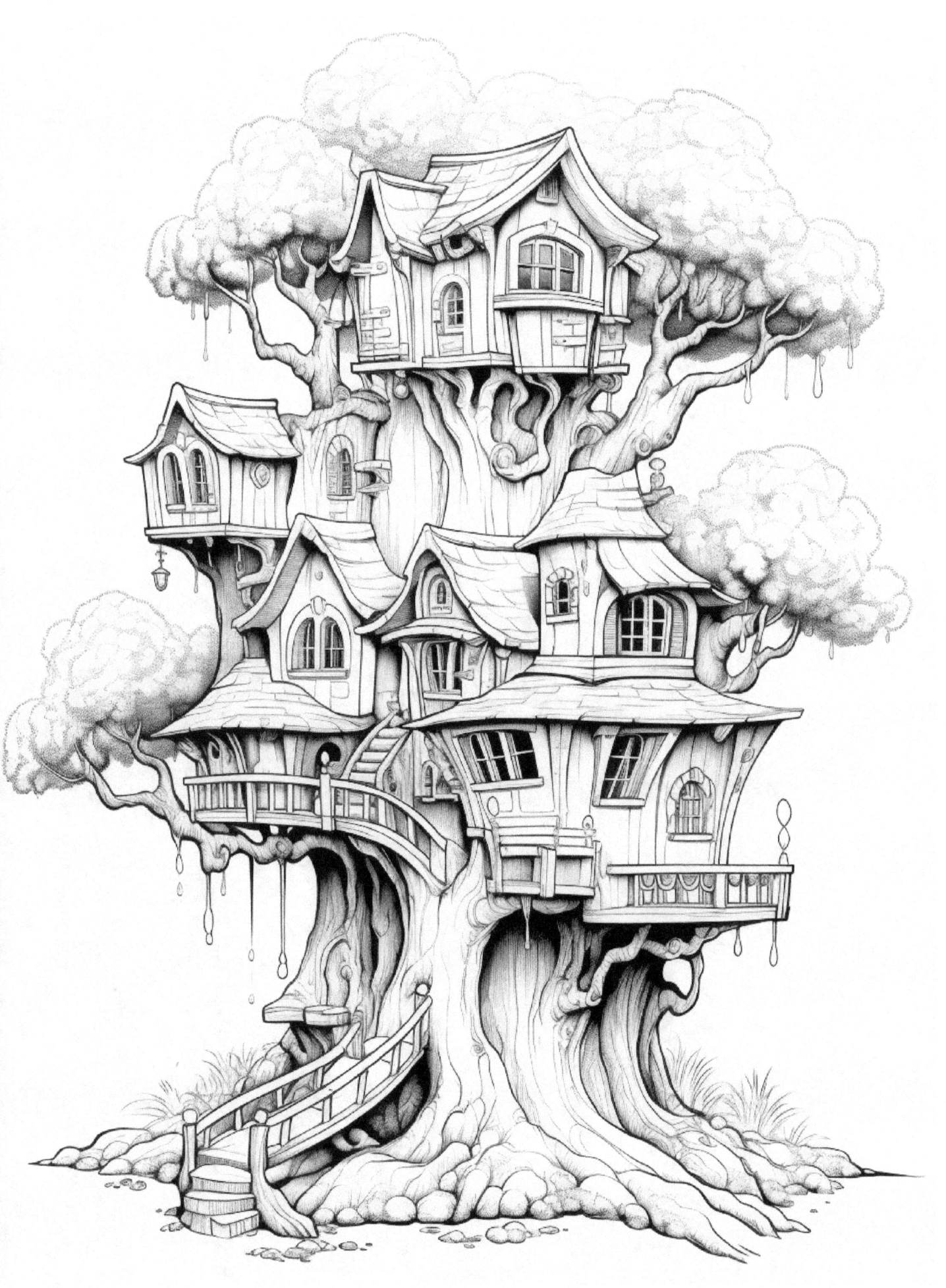

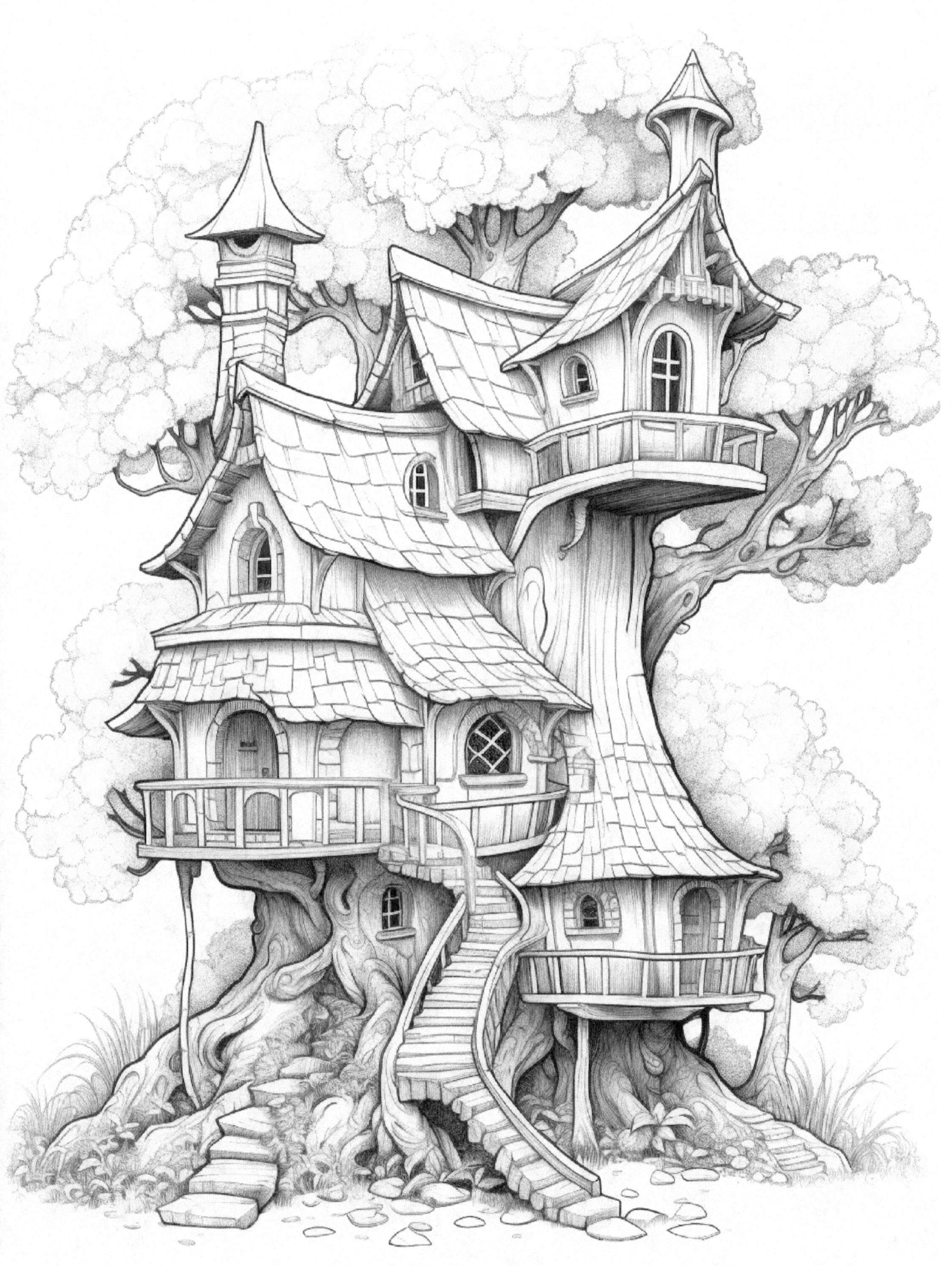

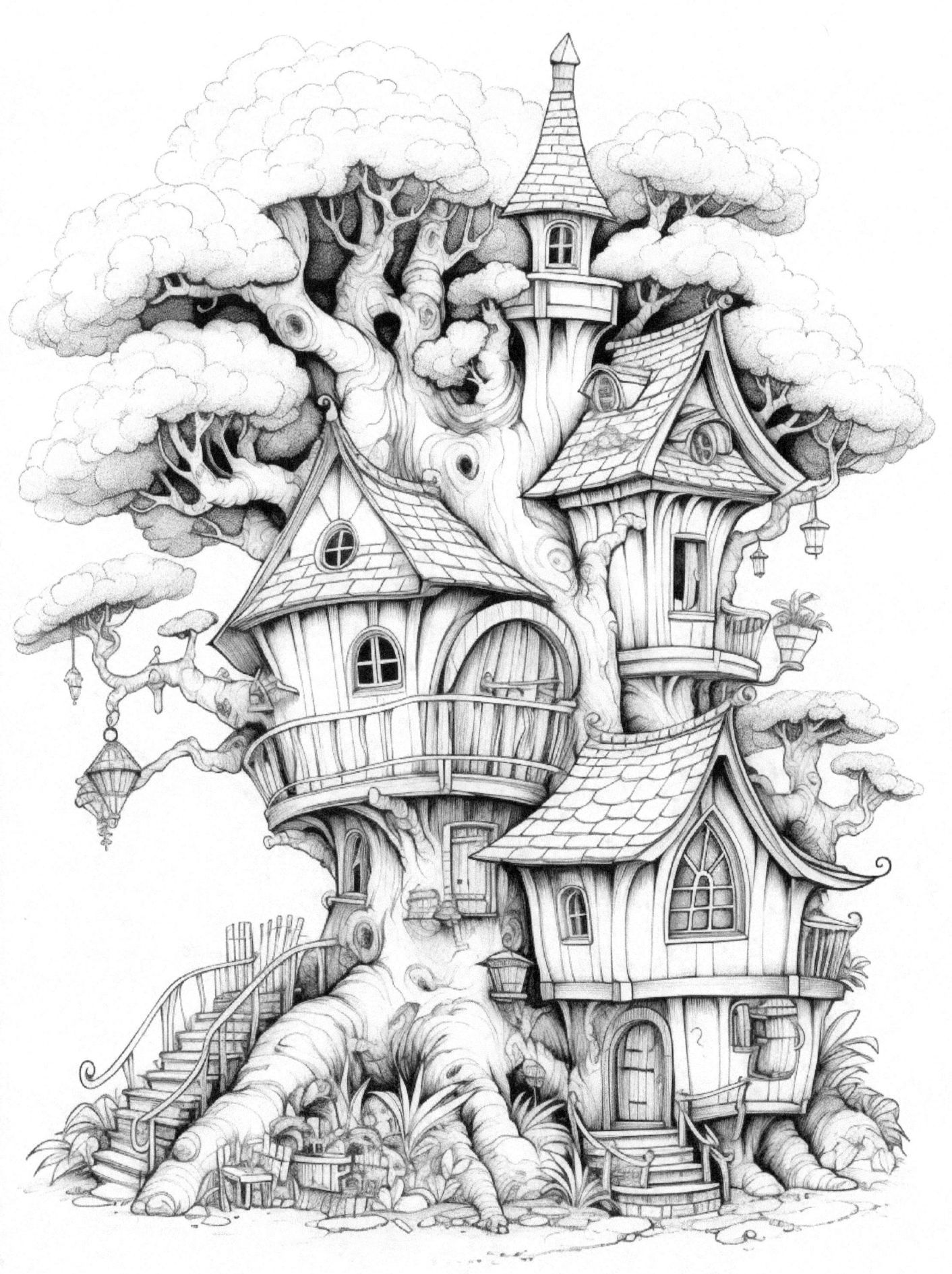

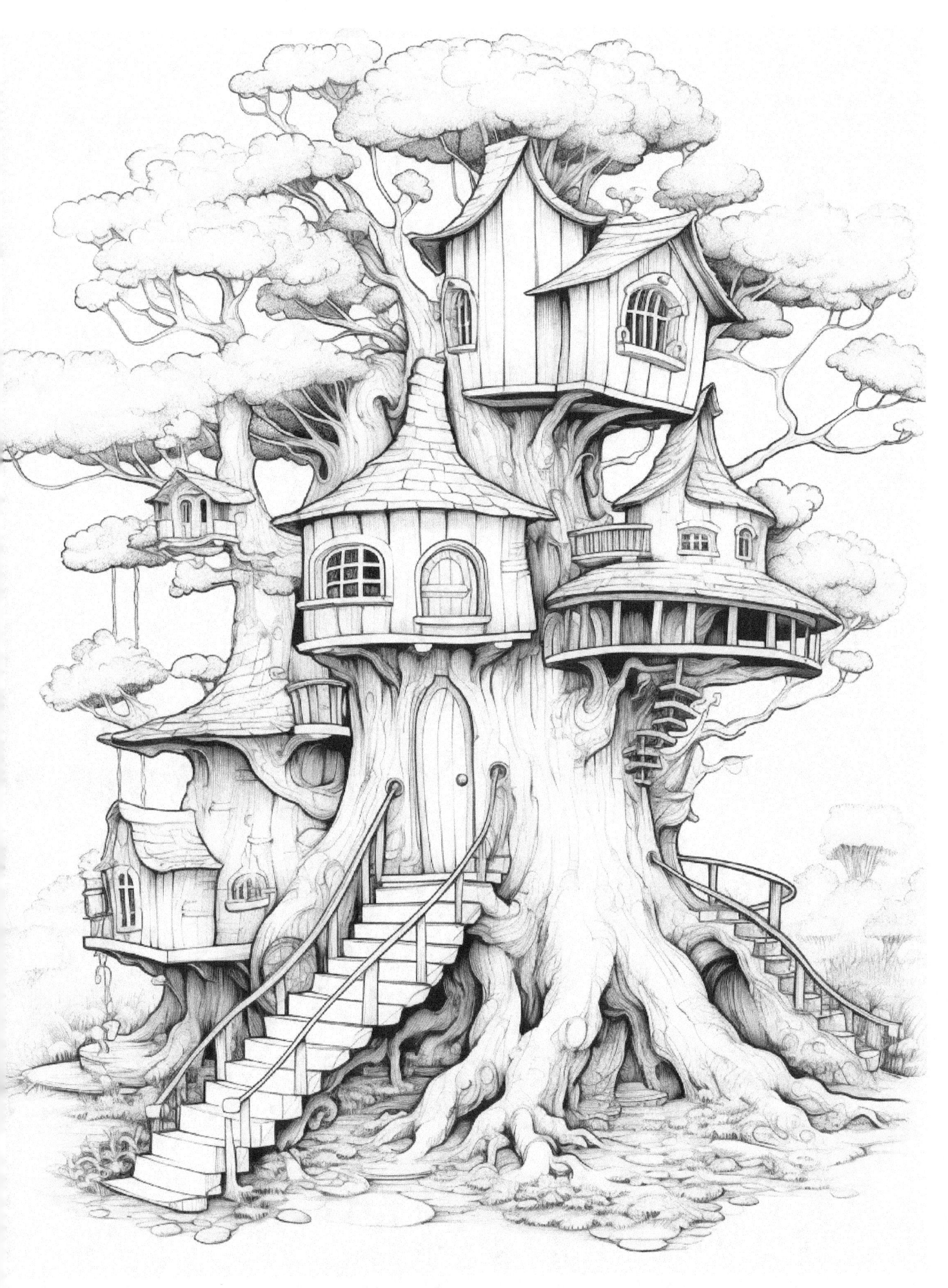

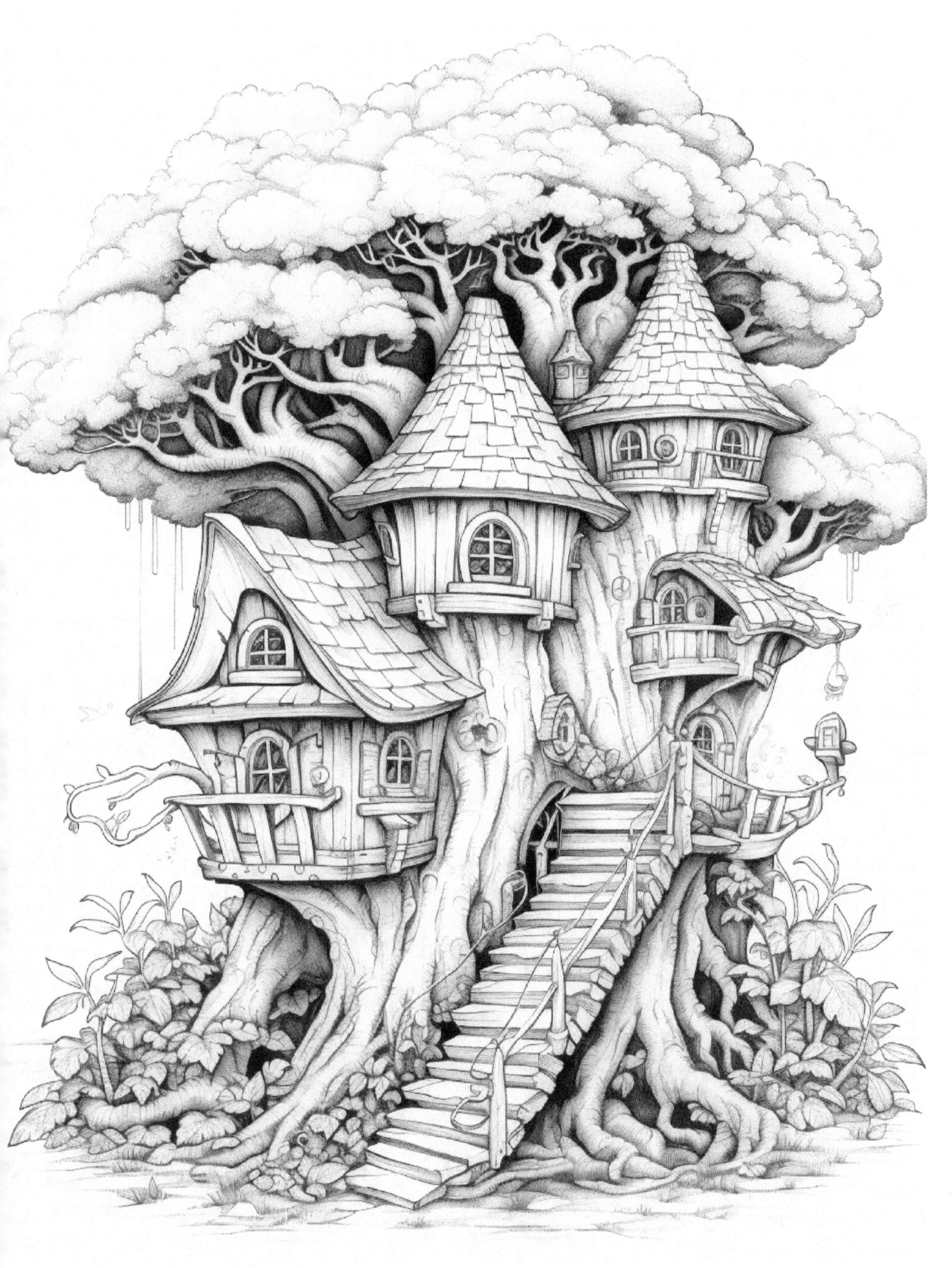

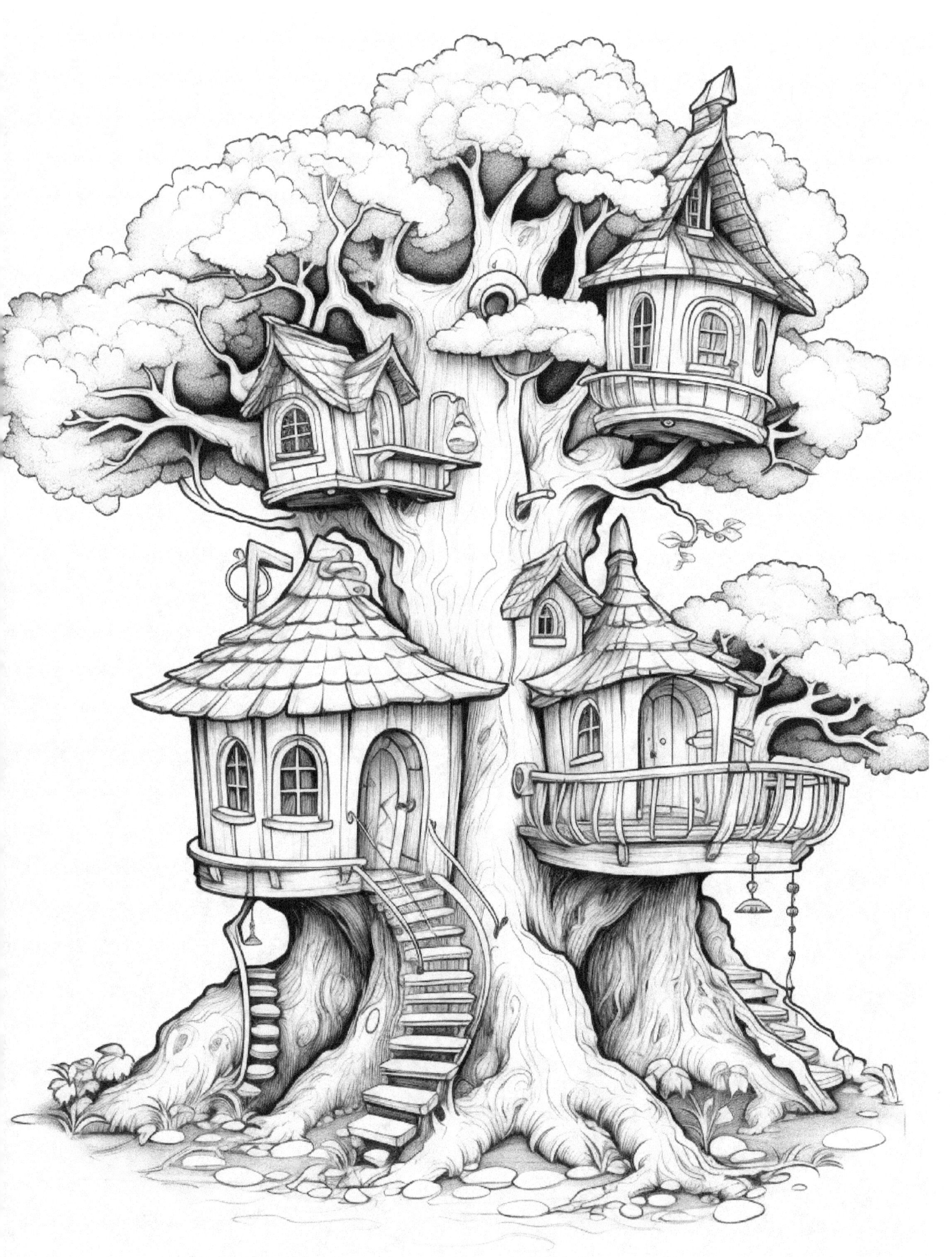

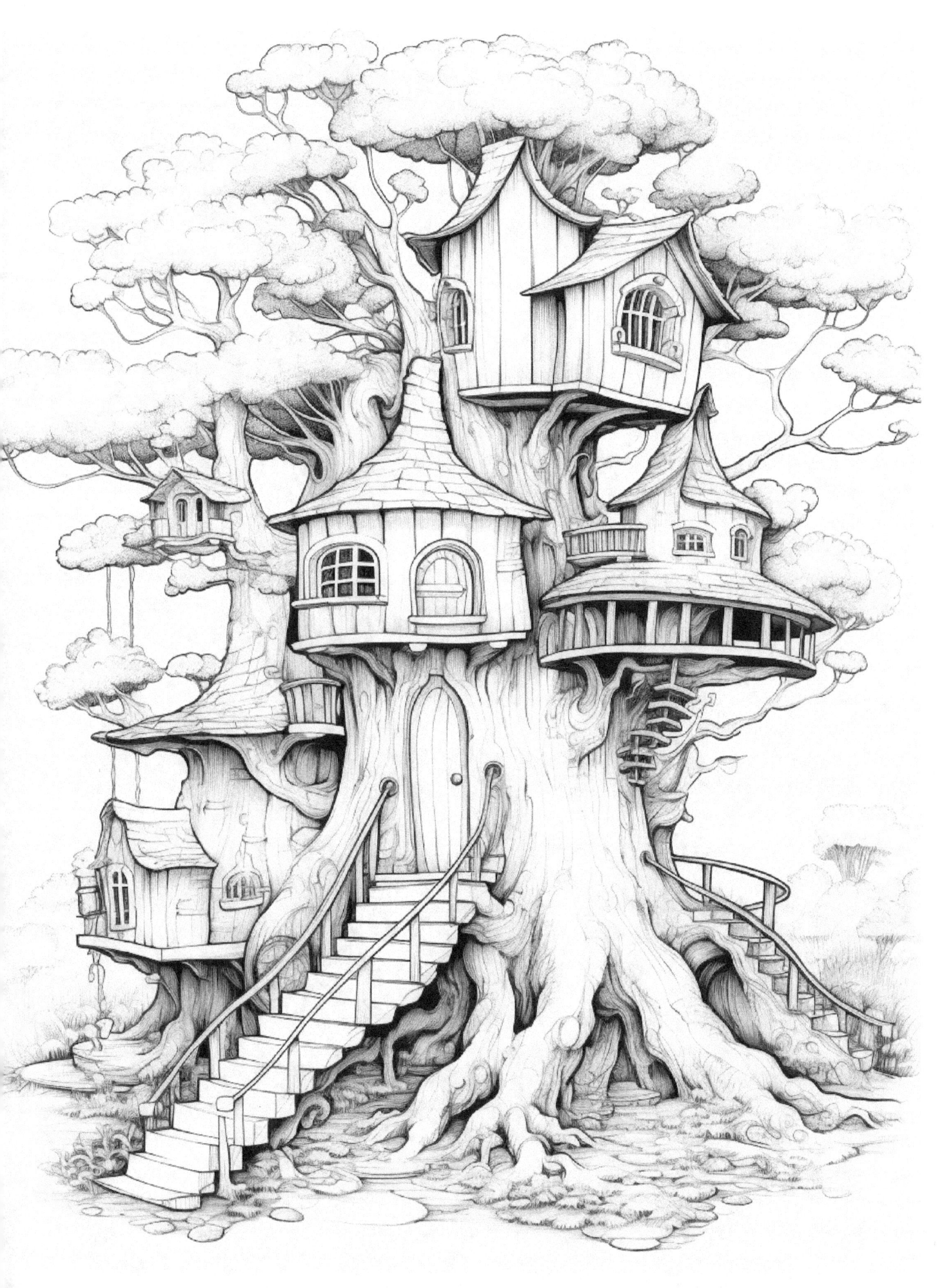

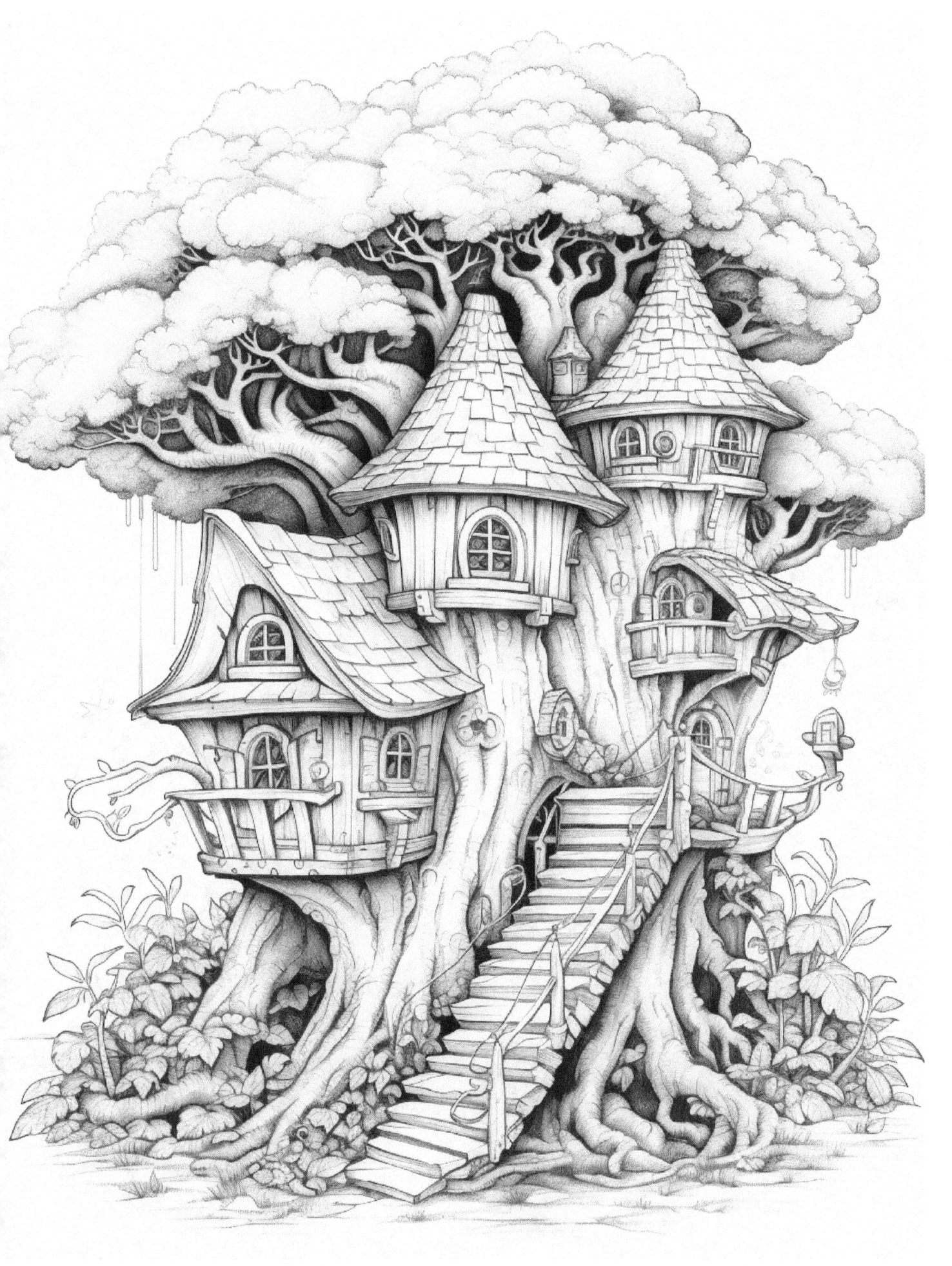

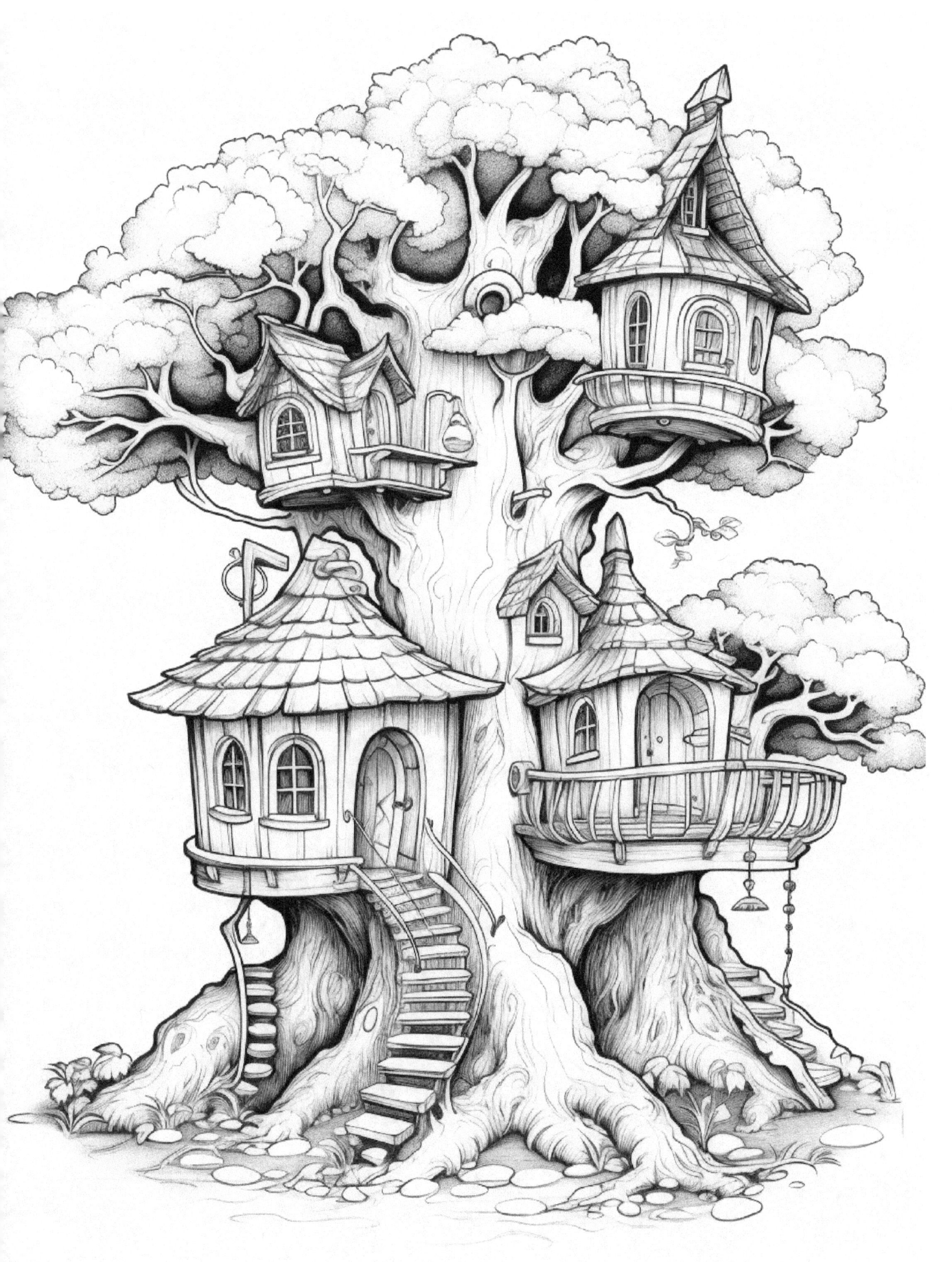

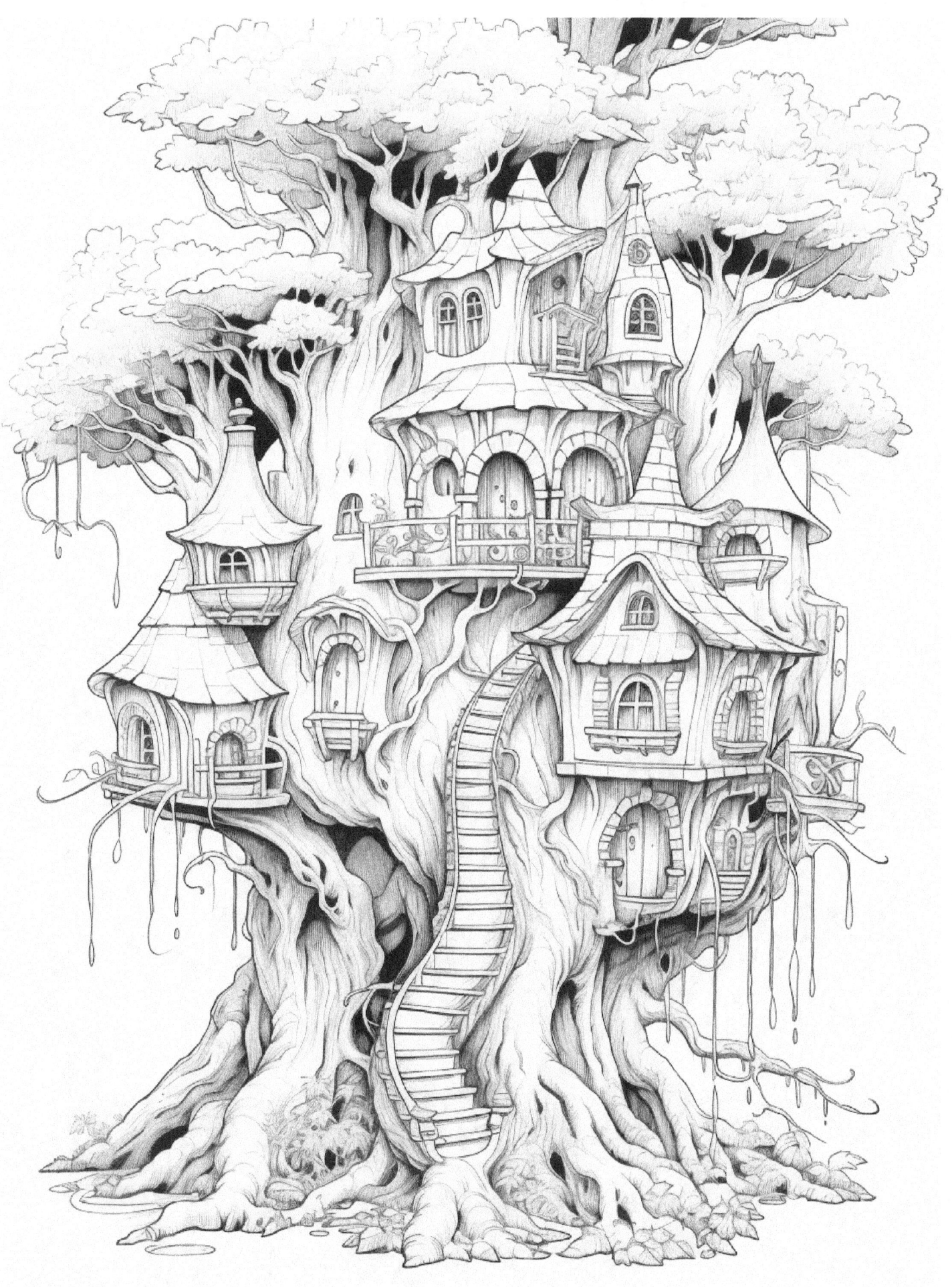

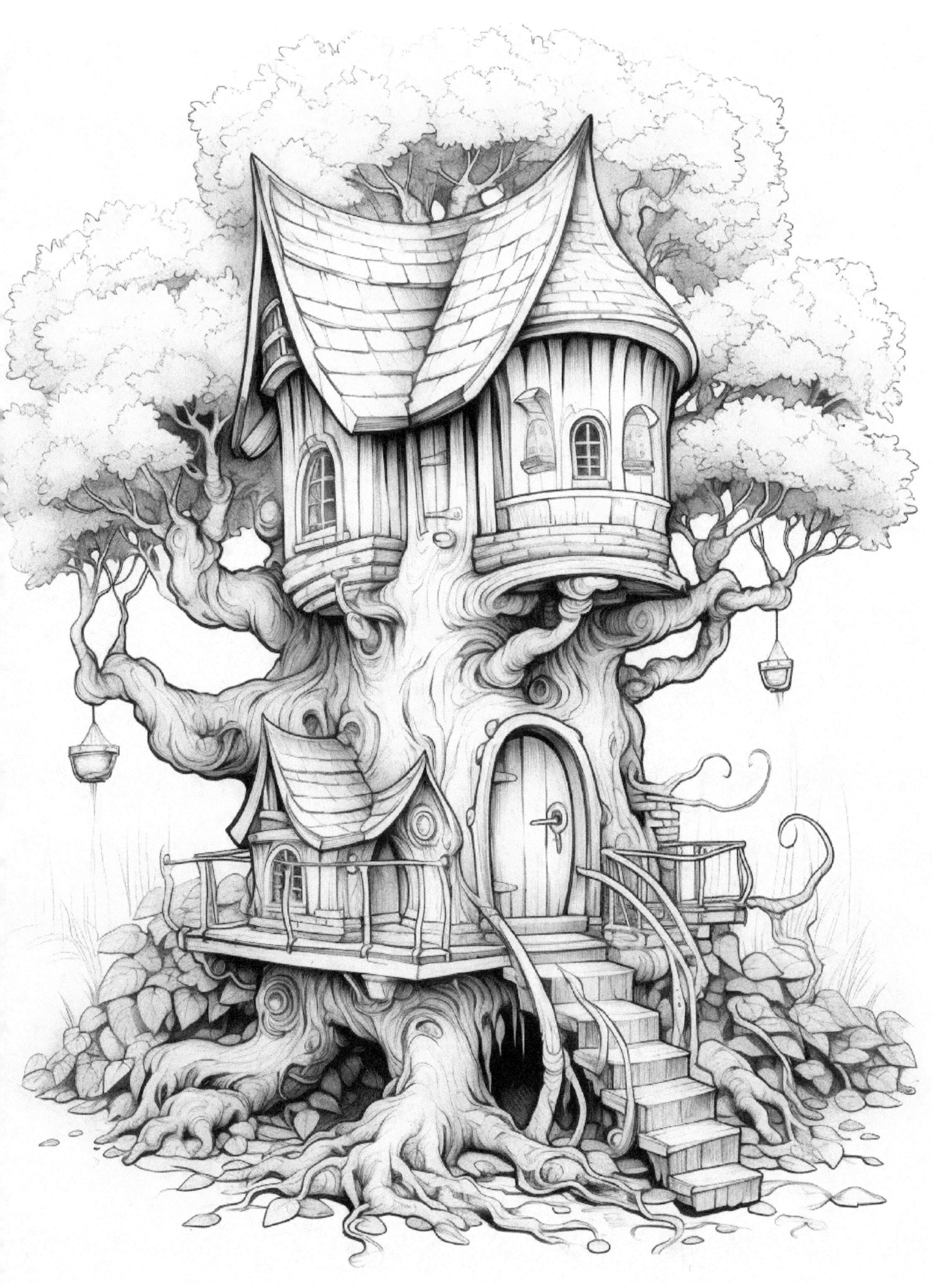

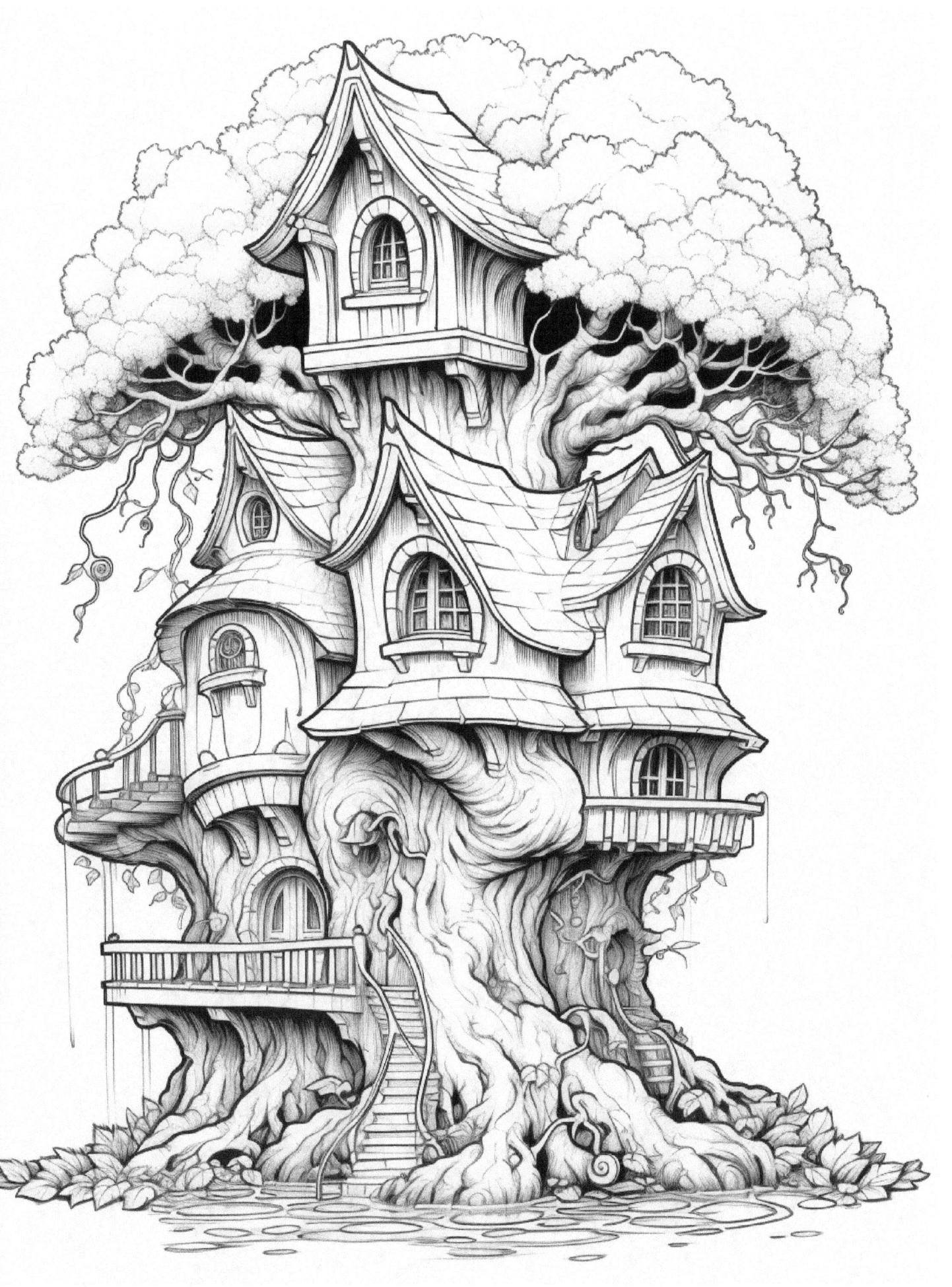

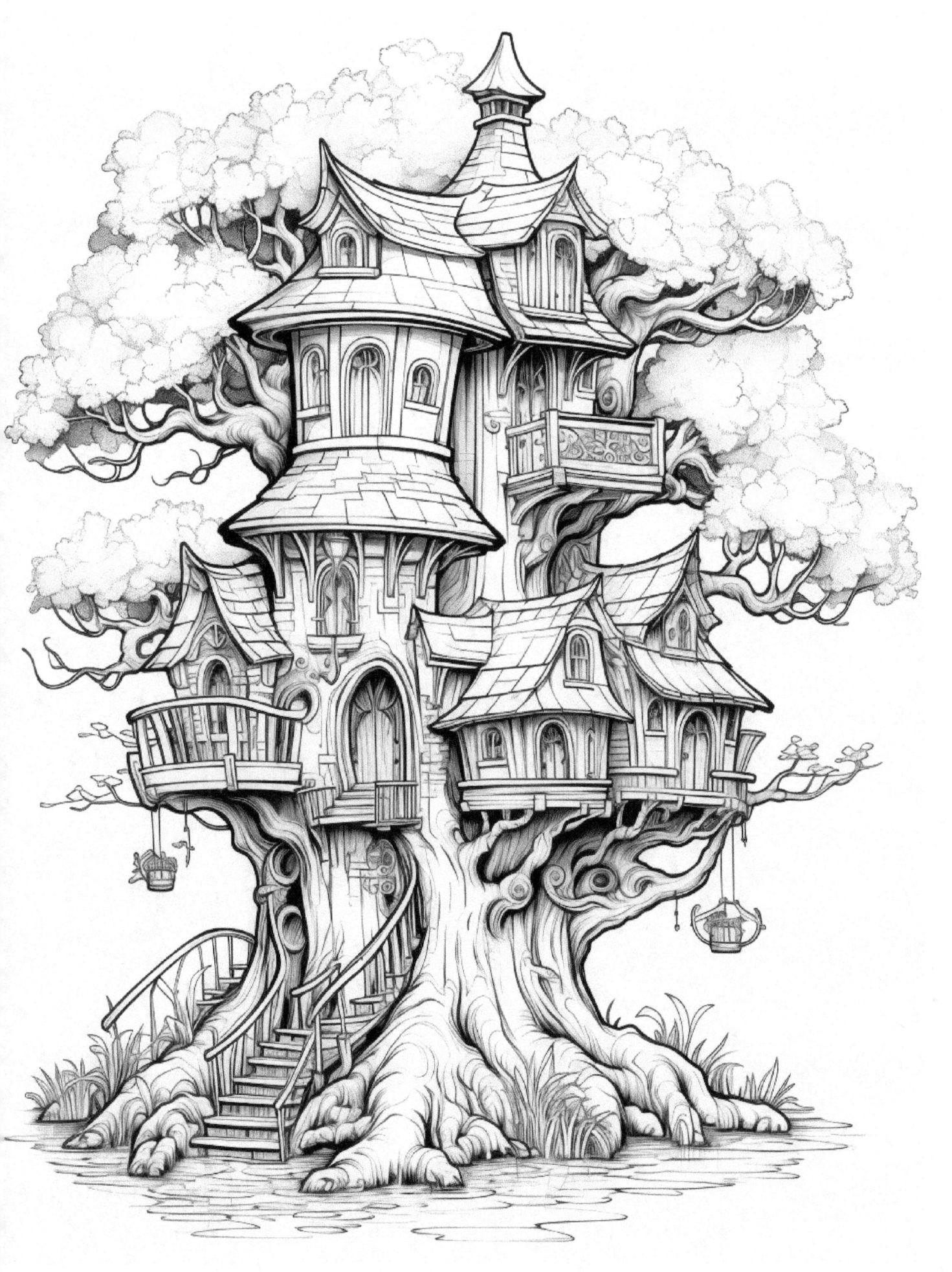

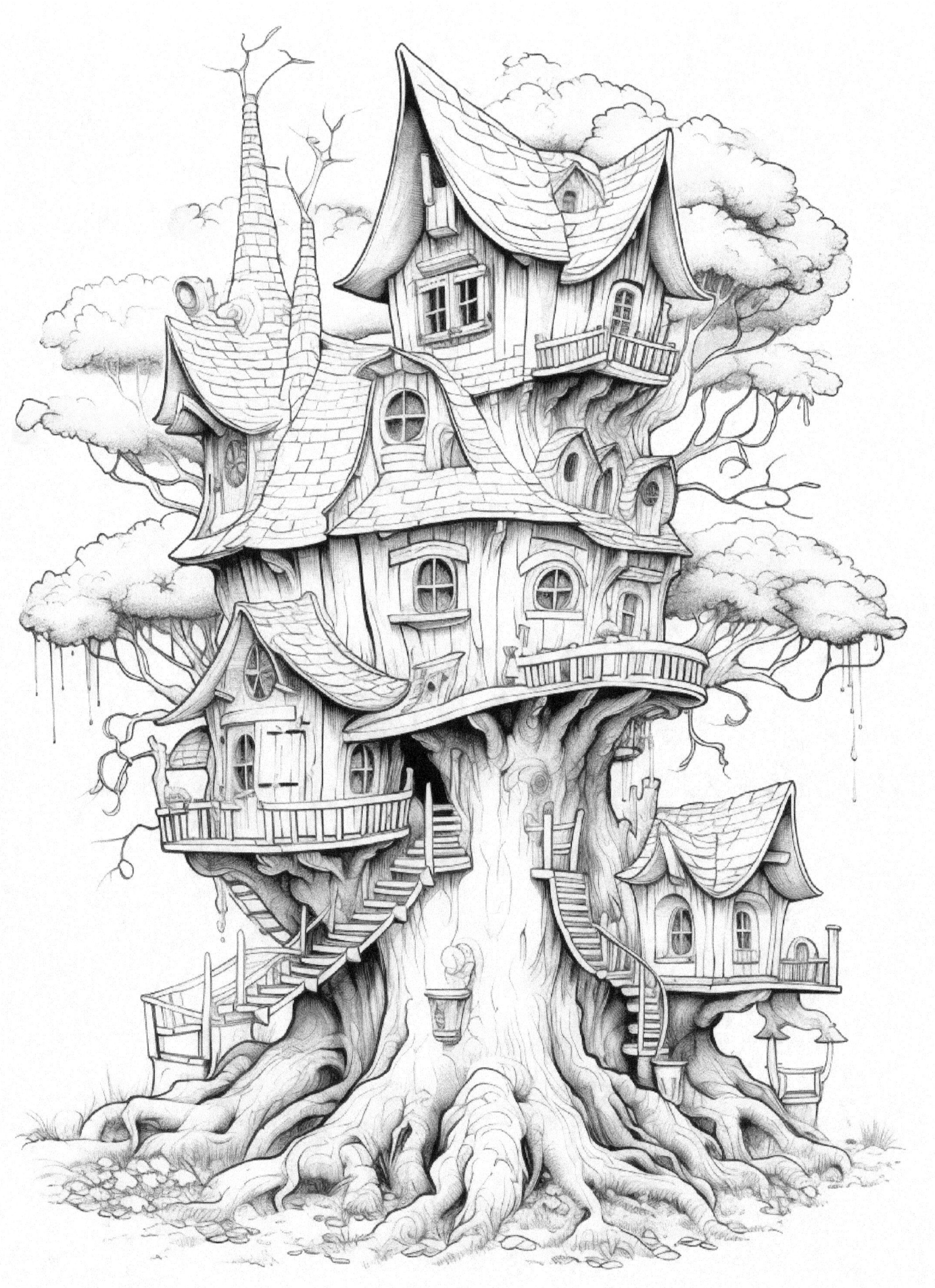

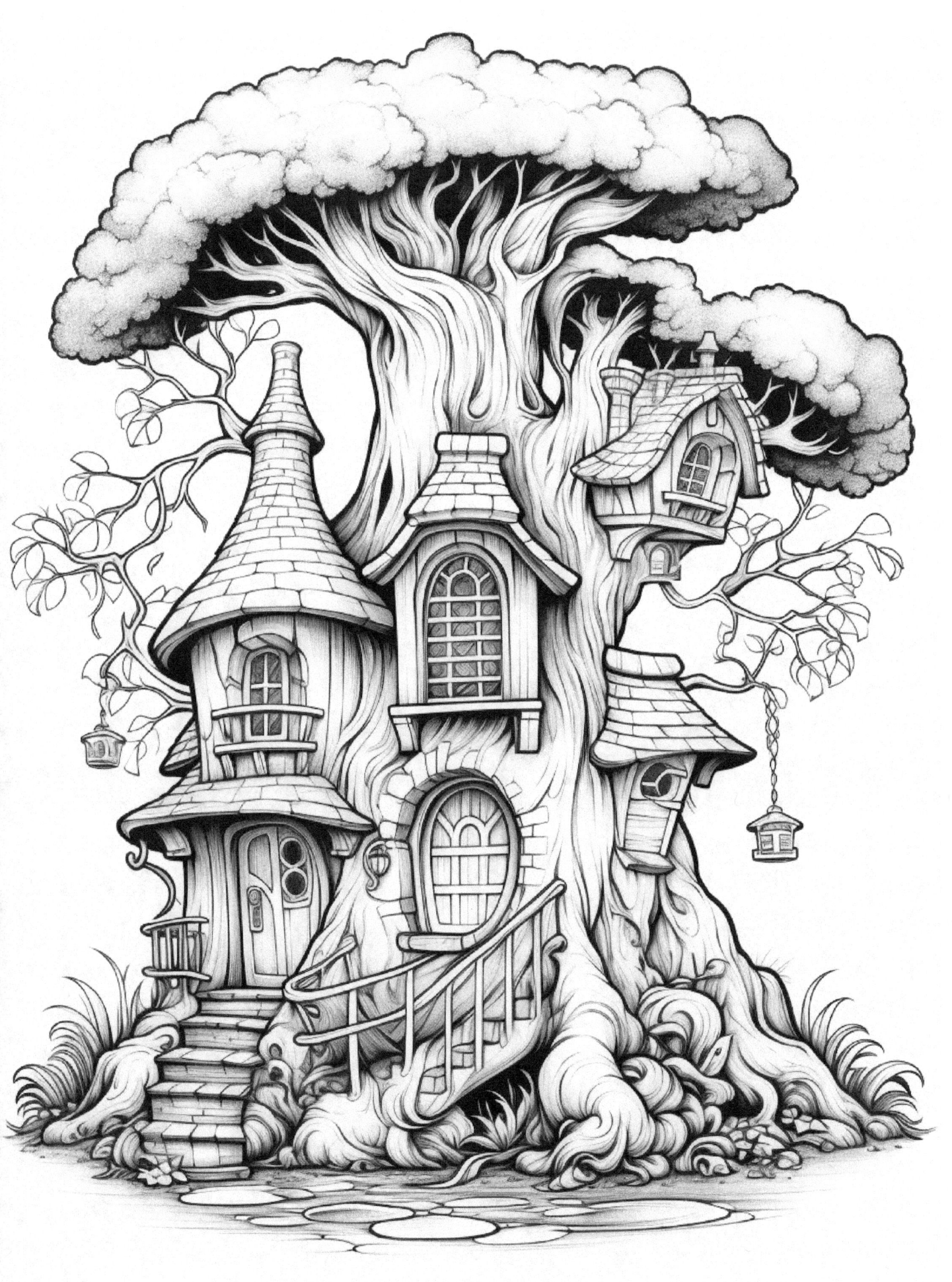

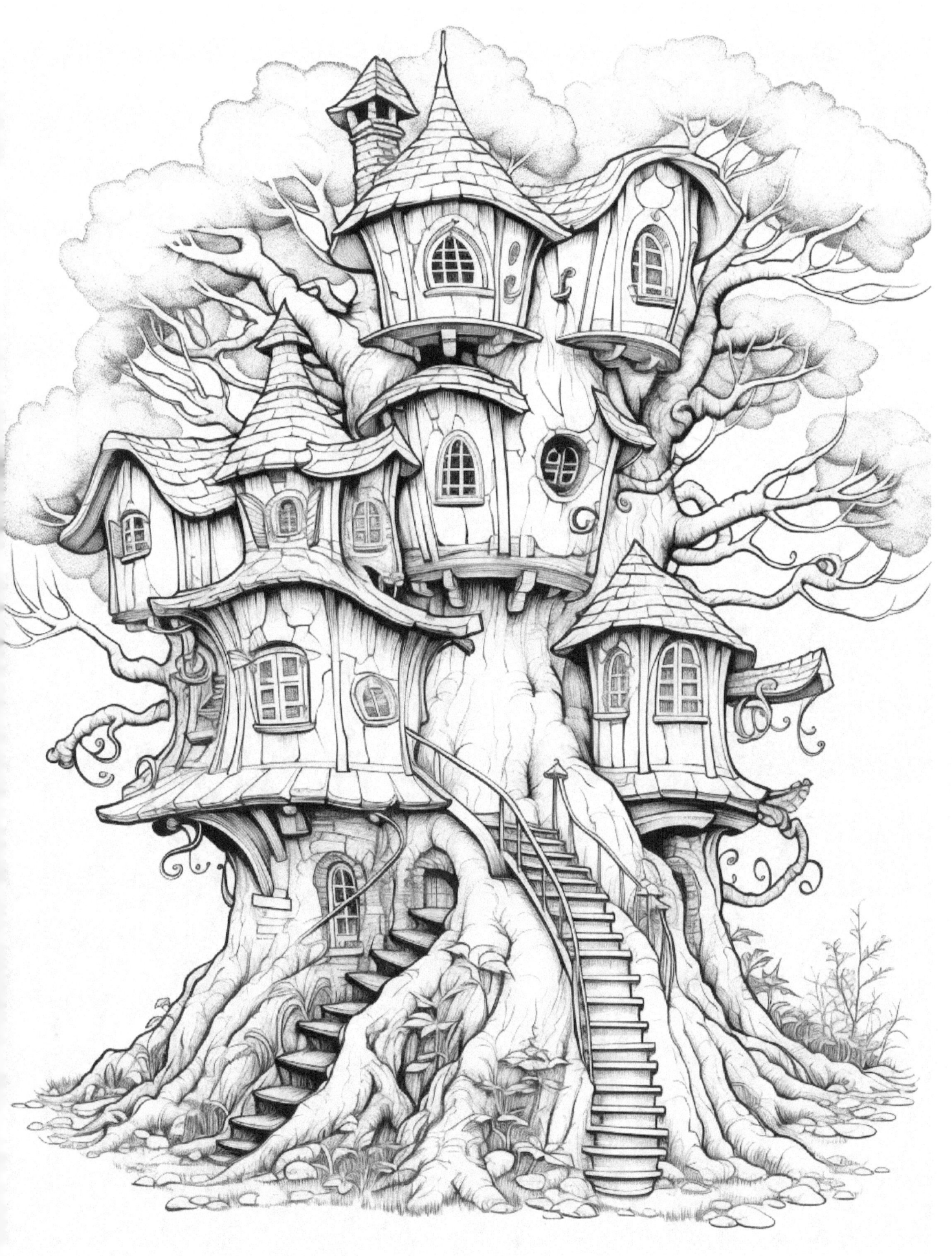

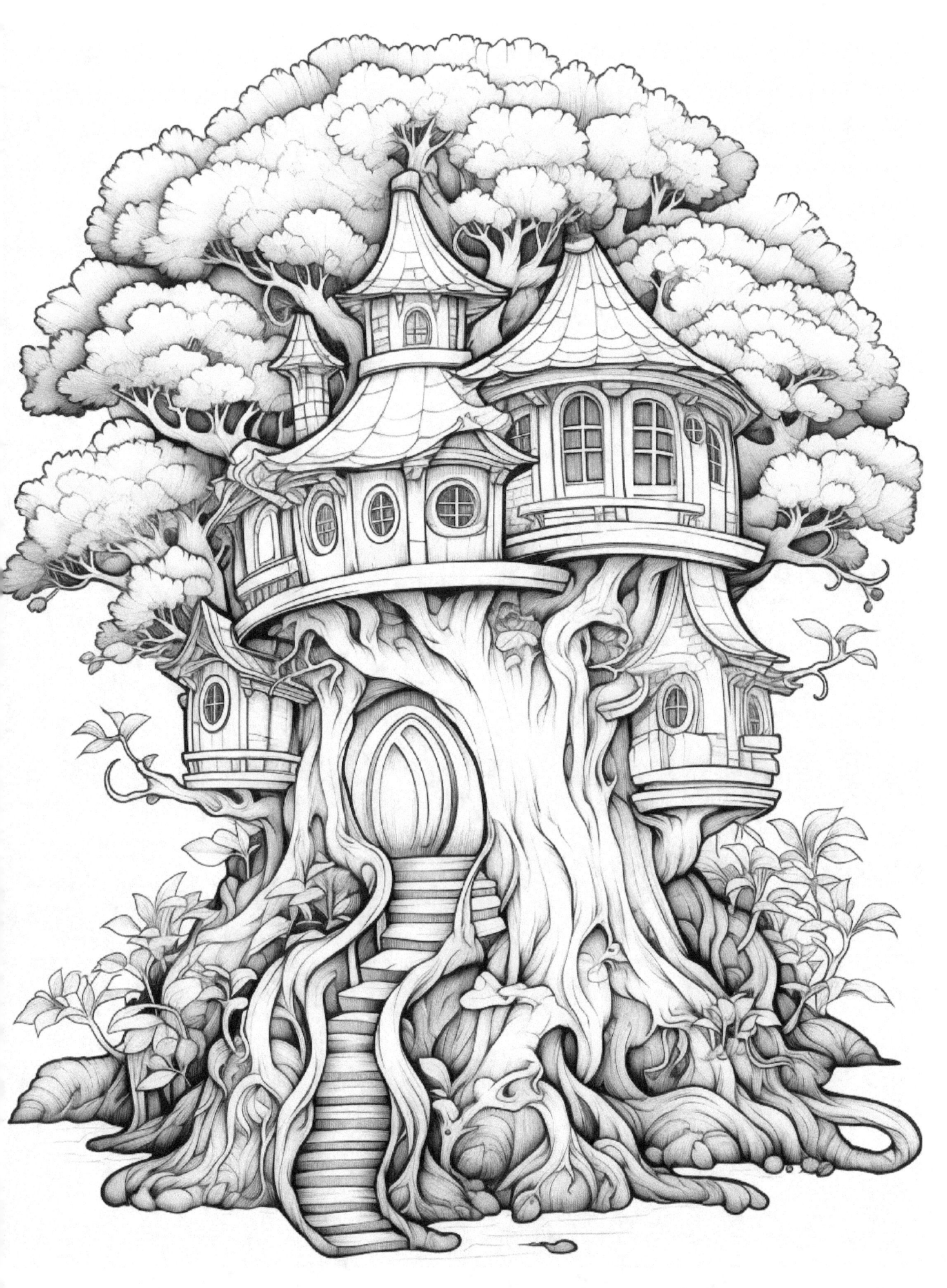

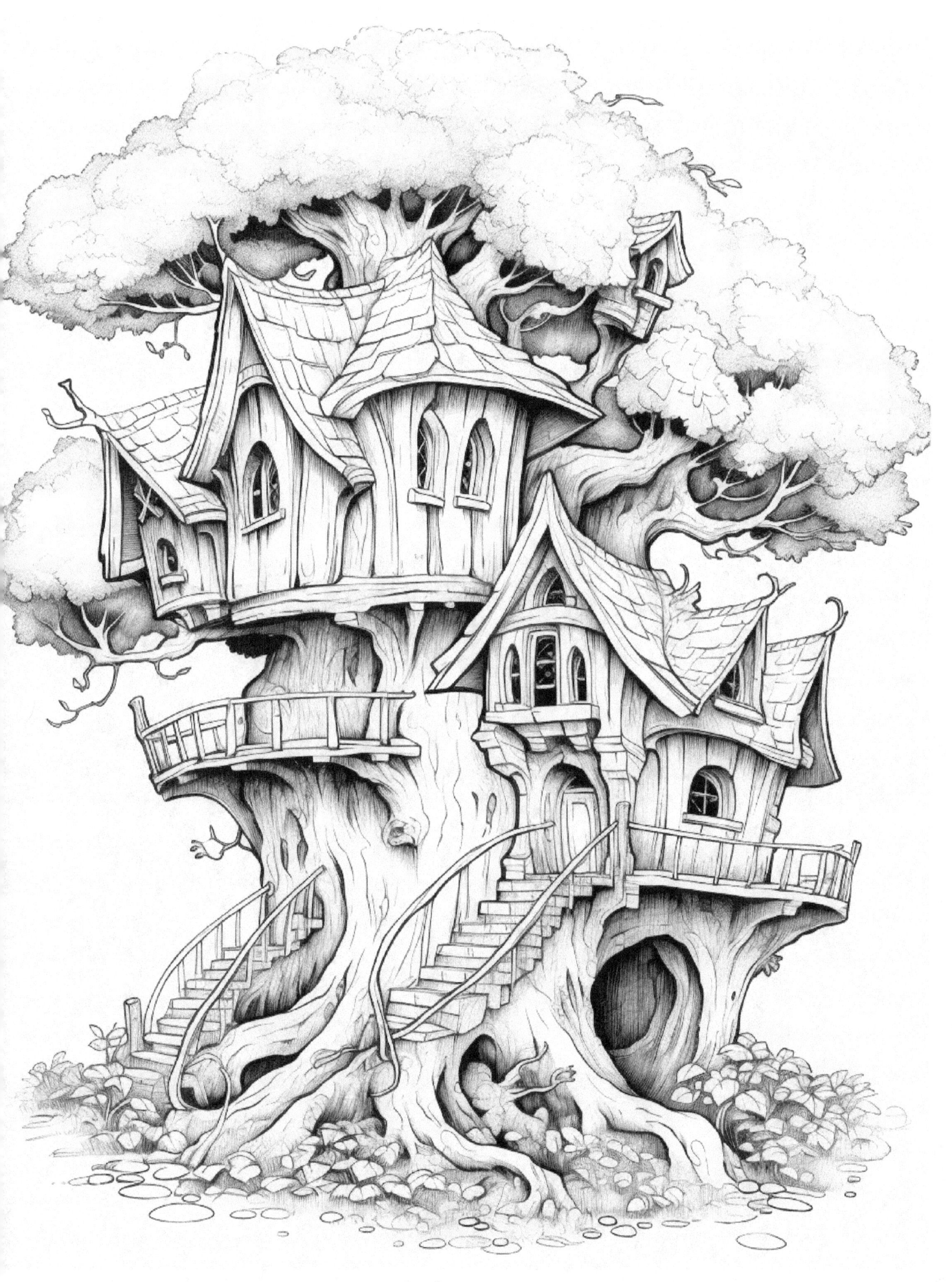

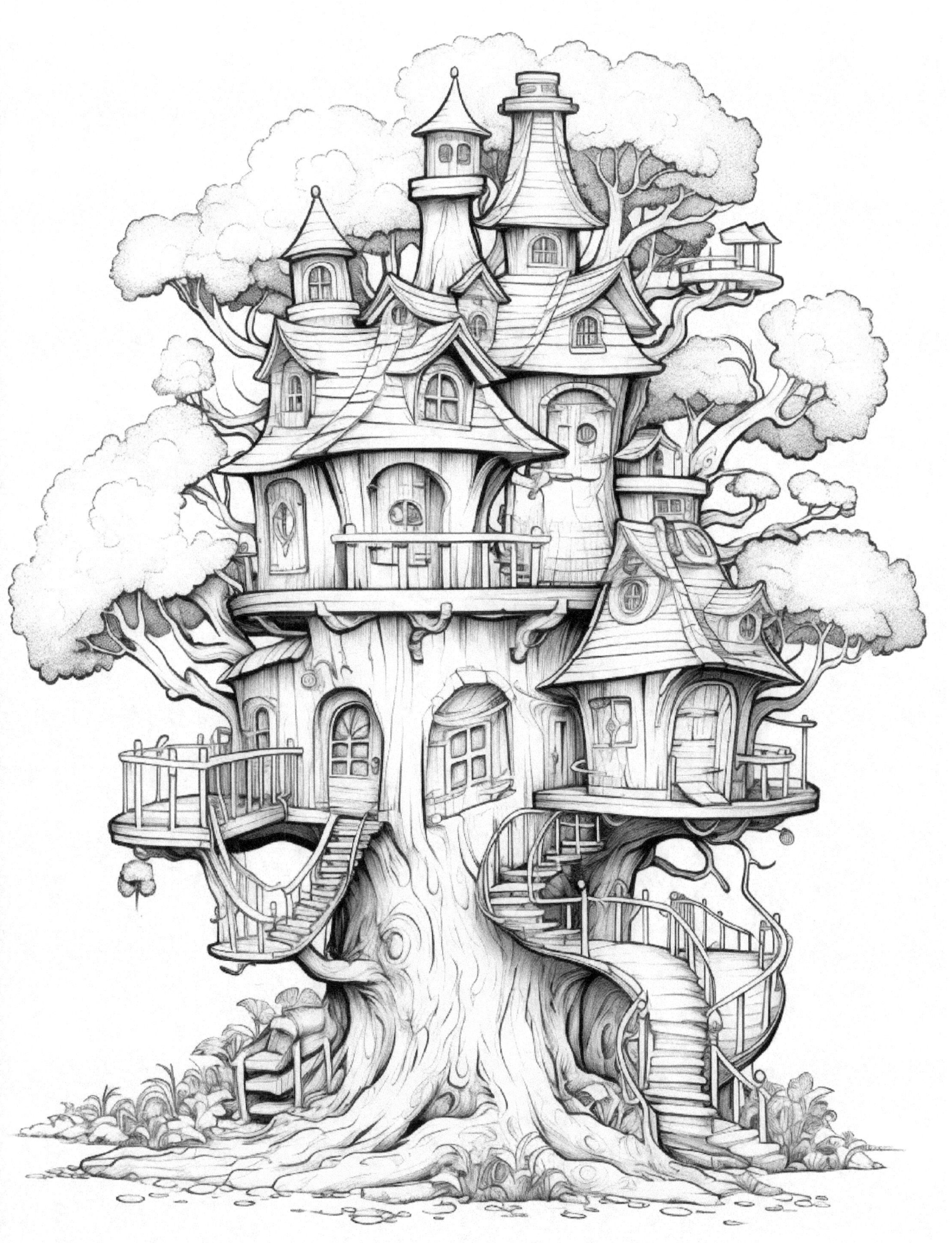

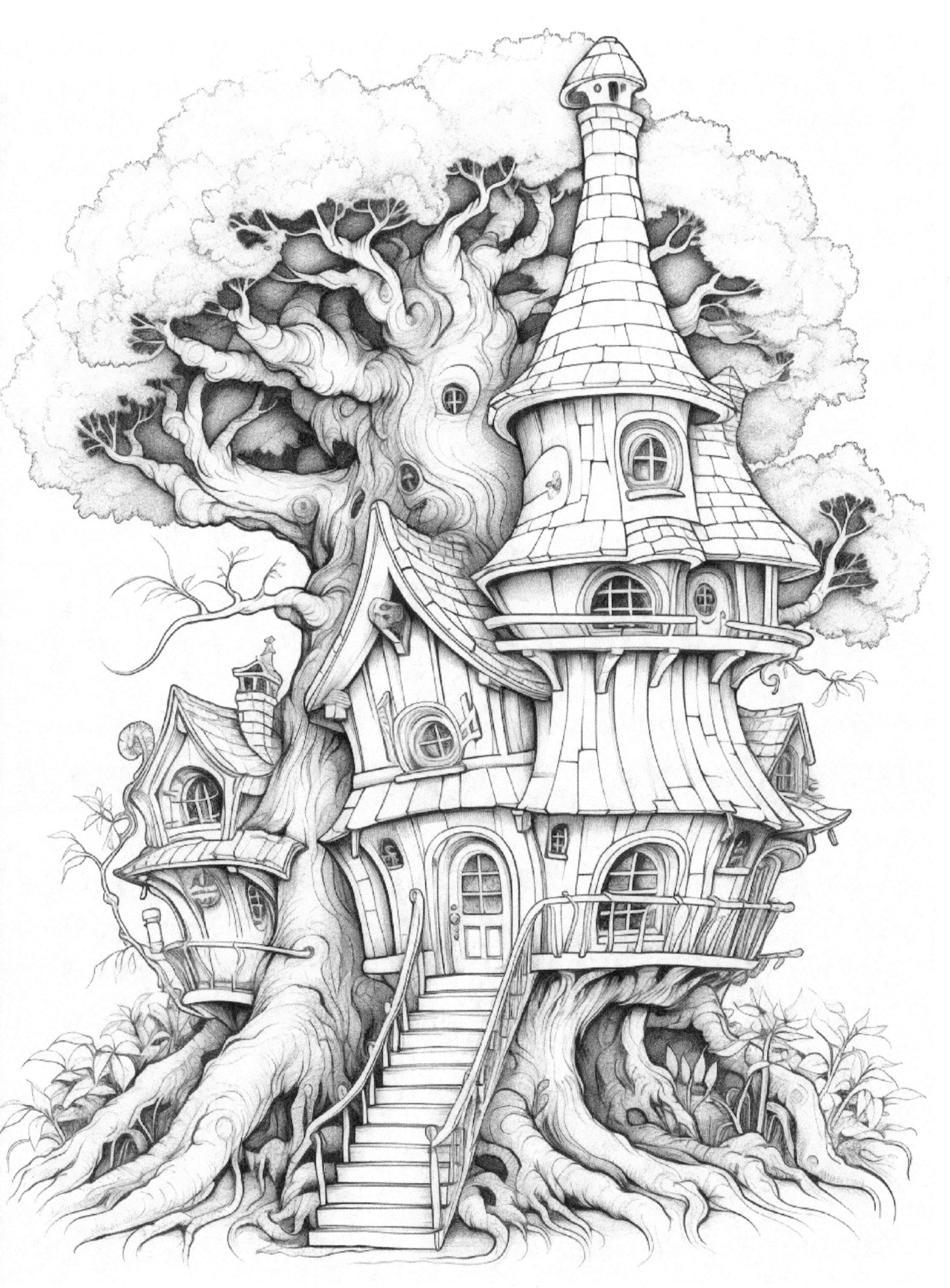

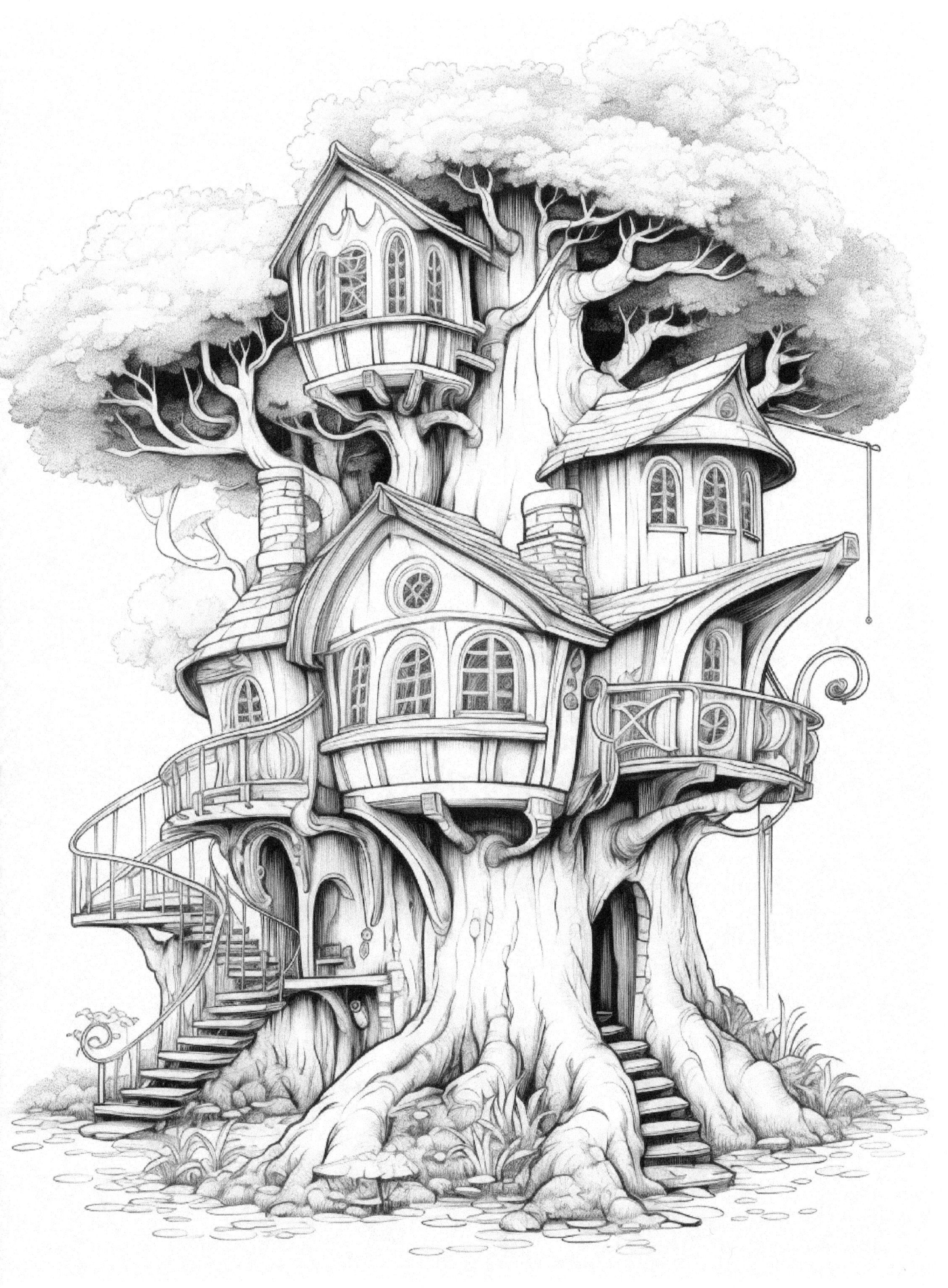

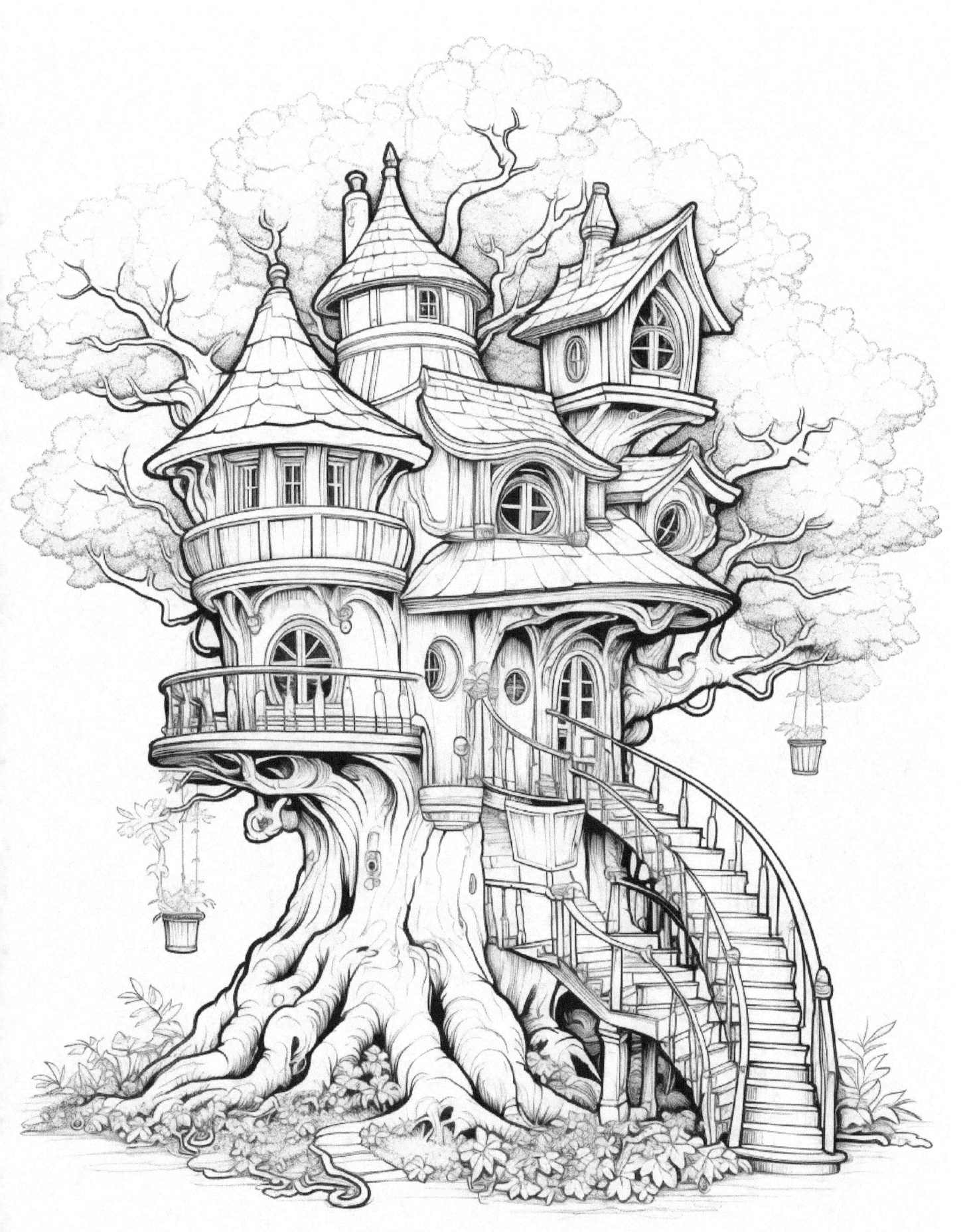

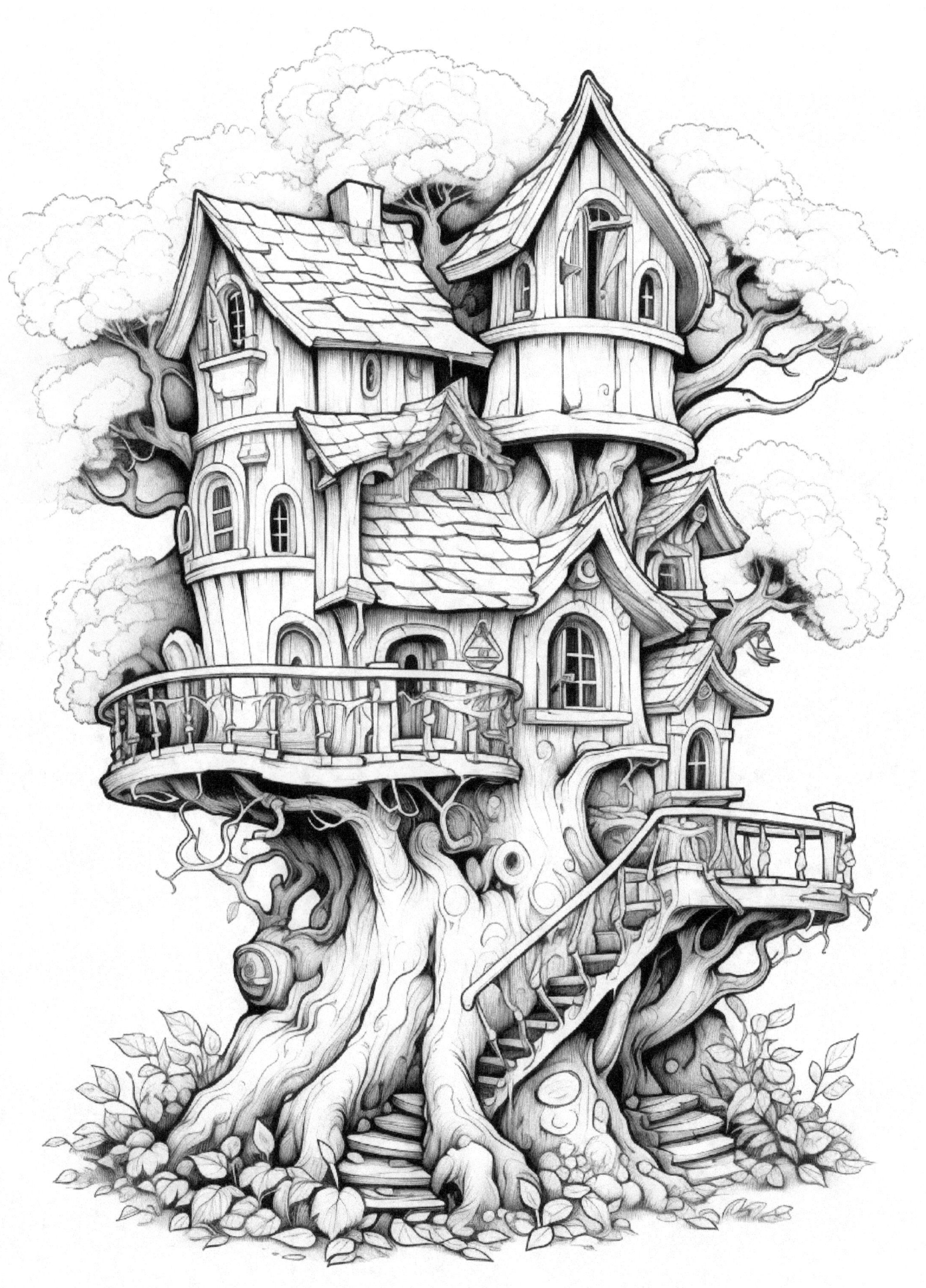

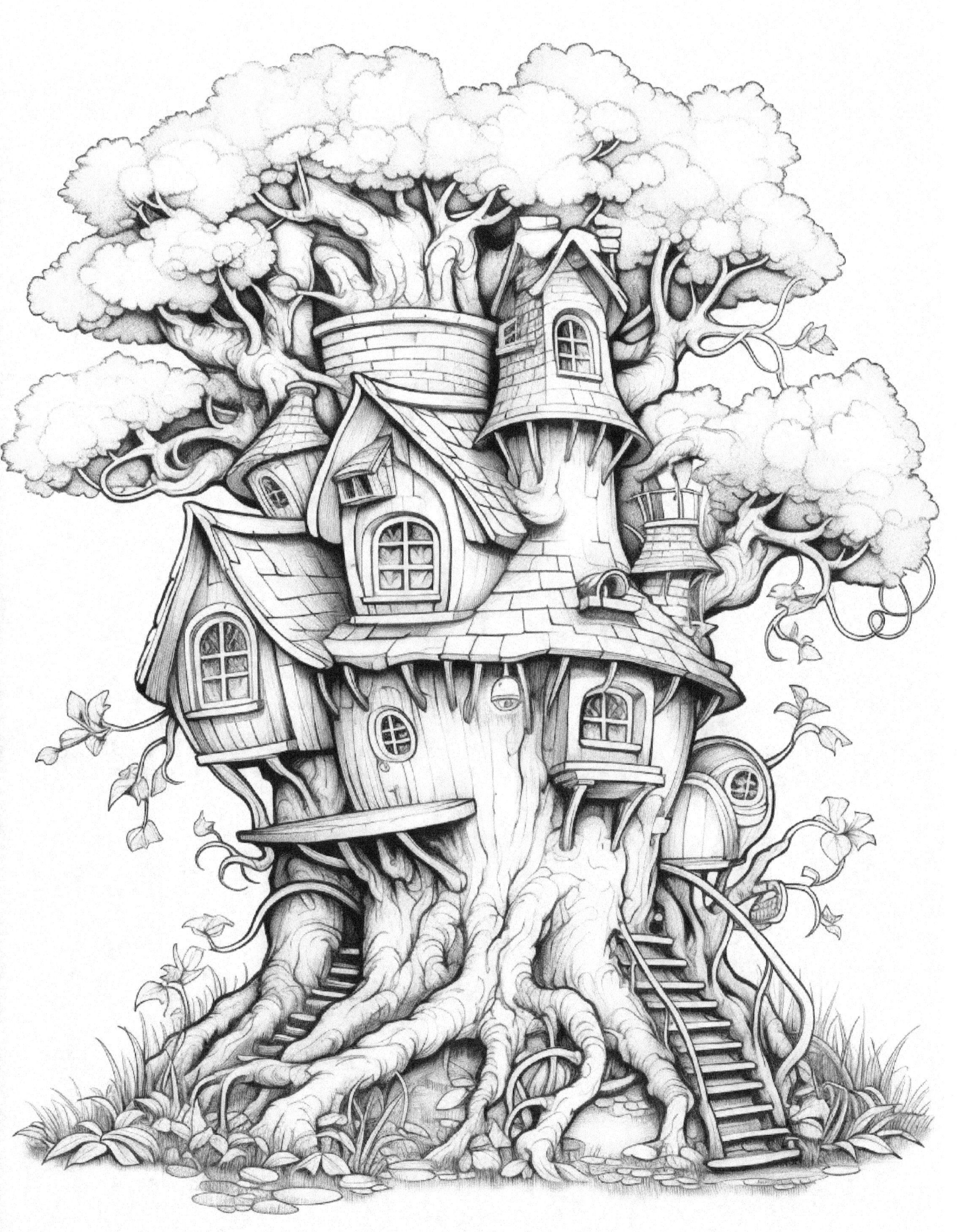

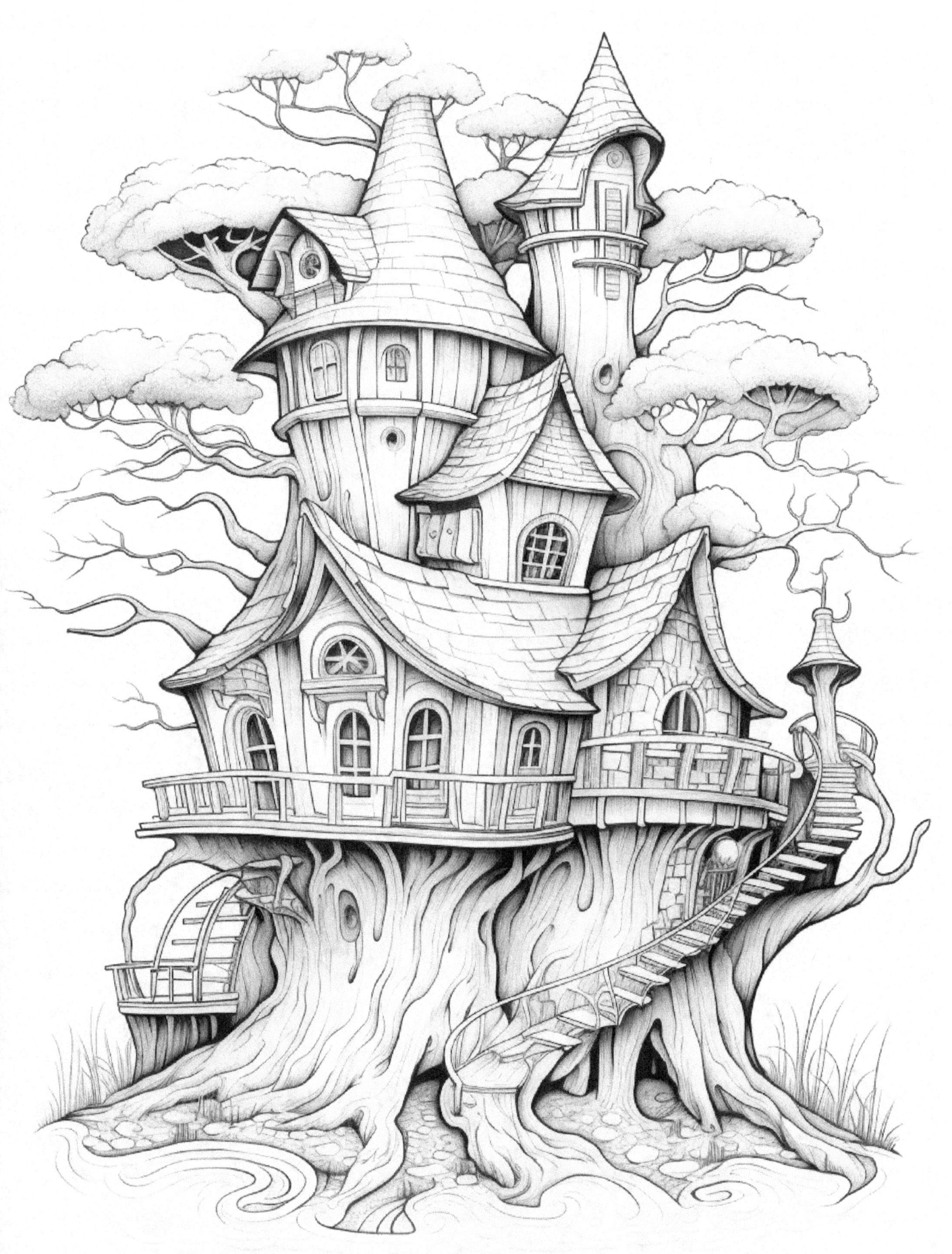

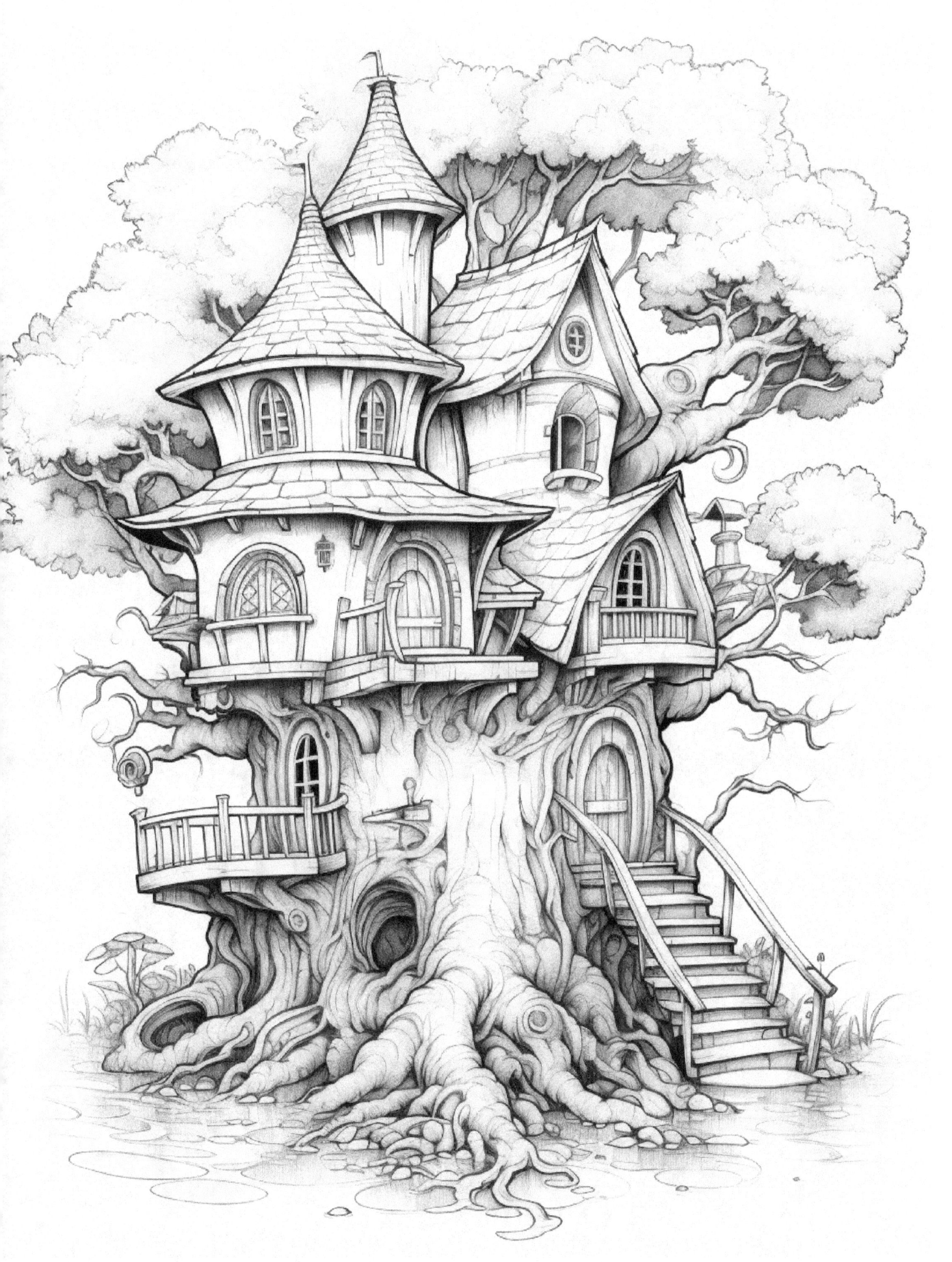

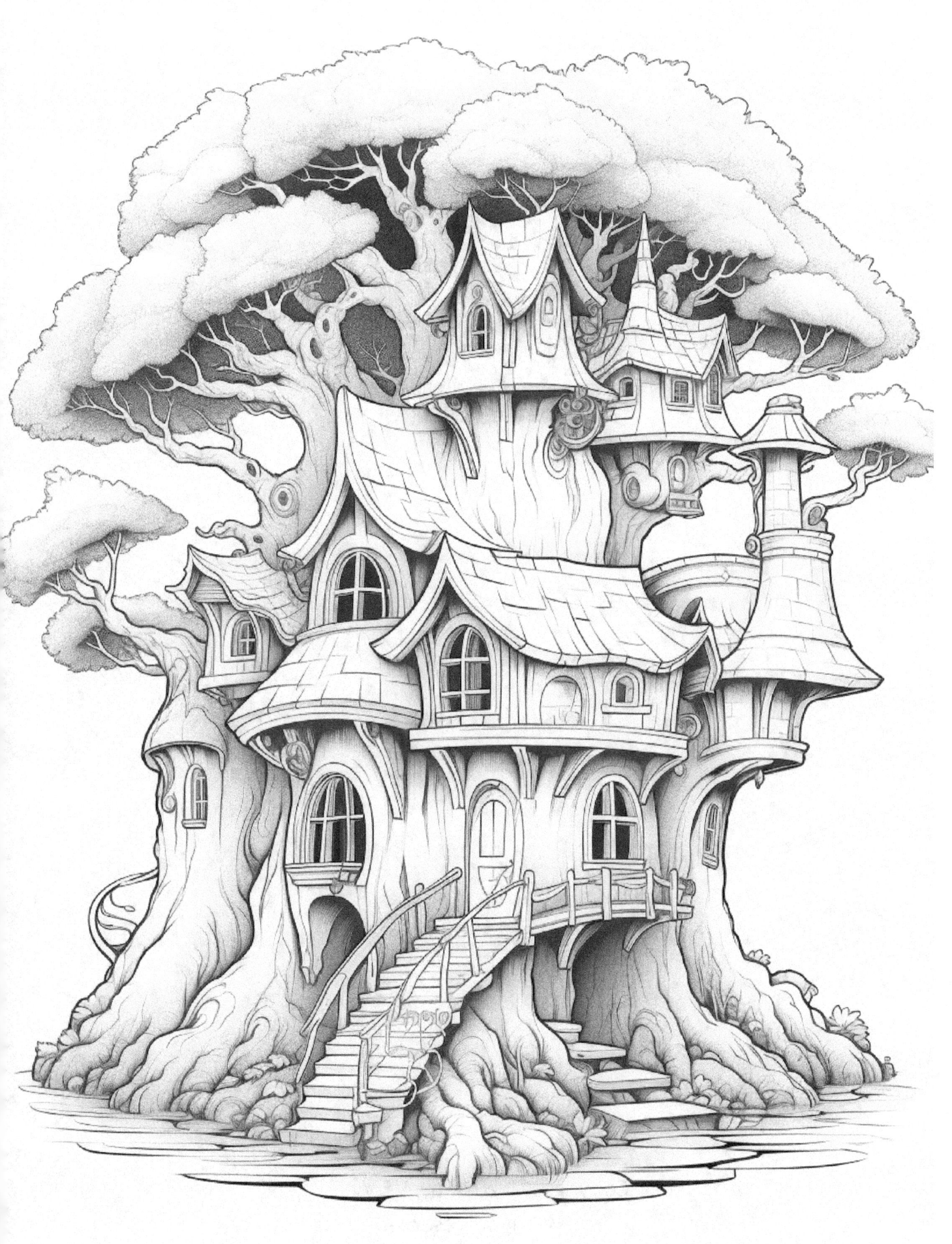

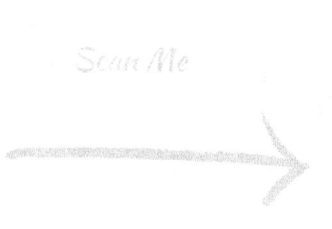

We appreciate you selecting our book, buying our coloring book, and helping our tiny business.

We wish you joy when coloring! We thank all of the contributors to this book for their generosity.

On our Amazon website, kindly post a review and some of your lovely colored photos.